A Video Arts Guide

So you think you can manage?

Video Arts

Cartoons by Shaun Williams

So you think you can manage?

Methuen . London

First published 1984
© 1984 Video Arts Ltd
Illustrations © 1984 Methuen London Ltd
Designed by Christopher Holgate
Printed in Great Britain
for Methuen London Ltd
11 New Fetter Lane, London EC4P 4EE
by Richard Clay Ltd, Bungay Suffolk
Reprinted 1987

British Library Cataloguing in Publication Data

So you think you can manage?
  1. Management
  I. Video Arts
  658   HD31

ISBN 0–413–57000–2
ISBN 0–413–56410–X Pbk

Contents

Introduction

I suppose it all began thirty years ago, when I was first shown an instructional film as part of my training as a National Serviceman. It was a comedy, and really rather a good one, telling us how young soldiers should (and shouldn't) behave themselves overseas. At the time it seemed just a part of the routine, but looking back many years later I realized that although I had forgotten most of what I had been told in the Army, I had not forgotten those short films, nor the lessons they taught; I realized that film instruction had a power and impact out of all proportion to the time it took up during a course.

The next stage came ten years later. I was researching management theory for my book *Management and Machiavelli* and was astonished to realize how many fascinating and invaluable lessons for managers had been worked over by researchers and writers. But even more astonishing was how little of it ever got through to actual managers. It was buried in such a mountain of waffle and pretentious jargon that most of it was effectively inaccessible to the people who needed it, even if they had had time to read it. There was this mass of management research on one side and a mass of working managers on the other, with only the thinnest trickle of practical guidance flowing across the divide.

It was a viewing of training films in about 1970 that brought together these two perceptions – the impact and memorability of film and managers' awareness of the sheer volume of practical help available to help them do their jobs.

The films I viewed that day were extremely dull and not very helpful to managers either, but the theatre was full of people from industry and government who were paying real money for them. I could not help thinking, just suppose the films had been full of the really useful knowledge that had been developed and tested by research?

And suppose they communicated those specific management skills I had so abysmally lacked as head of a programme department in BBC television – chairing meetings, negotiating contracts, selecting staff, carrying out annual interviews, delegating authority and all the other professional tasks which no one taught me and which I had to try to pick up as I went along? And suppose the films had been approached as entertainment, using high quality comedy or drama to put the lessons across?

That was the moment when the Video Arts films began, but I knew I could not go in alone. The three professional television colleagues I persuaded to join in – Peter Robinson, Michael Peacock and John Cleese – are still together twelve years later, and we have now produced more than sixty films which have been used by over 26,000 UK companies and in some 50 countries all round the world; they have won getting on for 120 national and international awards, including the Queen's Award for Export Performance.

The films are universally known as 'The John Cleese Films' and beyond doubt it is his comedy writing and performance that have created the company's distinctive reputation and given the films their unique impact. But in fact it is the quality of the teaching, the selection of key training points and the meticulous construction of the lessons that give them their lasting value. A twenty-five-minute film cannot teach much, so the training must be double-distilled to remove everything except the essence of the subject. Twelve years of this painstaking process have now produced, almost as a by-product, a whole corpus of compact, concentrated booklets for working managers expressed in simple language and designed to be an enjoyable read, now further refined into this detailed guide book on the essentials of management. A book may not have all the comedy impact of a film, but it can put in many of the important points that a film has to leave out, and it is permanent, portable and instantly accessible in a way that film or video can never be. That is why we are producing a series of books based on the films, of which this is the first: we hope it will prove a valuable and entertaining management skills manual for those who have not yet encountered the films, and a happy reminder, recapitulation and reinforcement for all the rest.

Antony Jay
Summer 1984

1 The unorganized manager, from damnation to salvation

The first principle of management is this:

If you cannot manage yourself you cannot manage anyone.

We are all familiar with the picture of the harassed, overworked executive: there is a mountainous in-tray; his or her appointments are double-booked; there is a bulging briefcase to take home after hours – in every way a suitable case for a coronary.

Yet such a person will have at least one comfort – they know they are doing a Good Job. The company depends on them; they are loved and needed by their colleagues ... But is this true? Let us start by looking at how one manager – we will call him Richard – performs.

Richard Lewis is in Food. He is an Area Manager in charge of half a dozen District Managers; but despite his responsibilities he never lets them get in the way of his goodwill, his ever-open door, his good intentions, his willingness to take on all problems, big and small. His behaviour is repeated countless times at all levels of all companies and organizations. Here he is at work with his long-suffering secretary Ginnie, and taking a telephone call from Bernard, one of his District Managers:

Richard: Yes, Bernard, of course I understand, yes I realize that, you're the Catering Manager ... well, why not mushroom soup *today* and tomato soup *tomorrow*? ... Good ... Fine, 'bye.
Ginnie: What's wrong?
Richard: I don't know, he always seems to need me to sort things out. Still, that's what I'm here for. Now, where were we?
Ginnie: We were doing this letter.
Richard: Ah yes, how far had we got?
Ginnie: 'Dear Mr Johnson ... '
Richard: ... Was that it? Right! 'Dear Mr Johnson ... '

So you think
you can manage?

But Keith, a colleague, rushes in. Richard
always keeps an open door . . .

Keith: Oh Richard – got a minute?
Richard: Ah, Keith. Yes, come on in.
Keith: You haven't got a cup of coffee
   handy, have you?
Richard: Yes sure. Ginnie, get Keith a
   cup of coffee. Me too, while you're at it.
Ginnie: Milk and sugar?
Keith: Oh, no sugar for me, thank you.
   Calories. Lovely girl. Very tasty.
Richard: Er ... was there something in
   particular you wanted, Keith?
Keith: What? Oh yes, yes there was
   actually. It's about my daughter's
   twenty-first birthday party. I'm getting a
   bit worried. We arranged that I'd
   organize the marquee and the suppliers
   say they can't do anything for that
   weekend.
Richard: Oh well, I'll see what I can do.
Keith: Great, thanks.

Richard, always willing, dials immediately.

Richard: Hello. Is that Under-Canvas?
   Yes, it's Richard Lewis here ... yes,
   that's right, I'm the Area Manager of
   Parker and Gibbs Catering. I
   understand there's a problem about a
   marquee for us on Saturday week ...

One of Richard's phones starts to ring.

Richard: Oh look – can you hang on a
   minute, my other phone's going? Hello,
   oh Bernard, can you hang on a minute?
   I've got Keith, the Vending Manager
   with me, I'm at a meeting and I'm on
   the other line – look, Bernard, I can't
   talk now. I'll hand you over to Ginnie,
   all right? Look Ginnie, can you take
   this? He says it's urgent.

12

So Richard has sorted out the soup crisis, is busy attending to Keith's daughter's marquee, left Ginnie to deal with Bernard's urgent phone call and, if he has time for thought, will be silently repeating 'that's what I'm here for'. Let's see what happens as Richard gets on with the job.

Richard: Hello, hello, you will do your very best for us, won't you? It's for Keith's daughter, you see. It's her twenty-first.

Ginnie: *Can't* you possibly talk to Bernard, he says …

Richard: I'll phone him back later, I told you.

Ginnie: Bernard, he says he'll phone you back. I'm sorry. 'Bye.

Richard: She's called Karen, yes, she's a sweet kid … Yes, so I'll be hearing from you then? Oh, they've hung up! Well I think it'll be all right, Keith.

Keith: Oh great. Thanks, Richard.

Ginnie: Bernard's got a crisis down at Bexley.

Richard: What sort of crisis?

Ginnie: Meat deliveries haven't arrived, staff haven't turned up and he's discovered some pilfering.

Richard: Oh Lord! Well what did you say?

Ginnie: I said I'd tell you.

Richard: … Well, is that all?

Ginnie: What else? I tried …

Richard: What else? Ginnie have I got to do *everything*? Sorry, I didn't mean to snap. Get him on the phone, will you?

Keith: Well, I think I'd better leave you to it then. Thanks for coffee.

Keith leaves the scene of confusion, oblivious to the fact that his request has helped to create it. After all, it's always like that in Richard's office. Of course several

13

vital things have been accomplished that afternoon: the colour of tomorrow's soup has been agreed; some progress on the marquee is in train; a nice cup of coffee has been drunk. Naturally one or two matters have unavoidably been left in the air ...

Richard: What's happening?

Ginnie: No reply.

Richard: Why doesn't he reply? Bernard can't blow his nose without consulting me.

Ginnie: He said he *had* to talk to you because he can't sack one of the kitchen porters for pilfering without your OK.

Richard: Oh. I see. Still no reply? Well look, you'd better trot off now. But try and get this call through to Bernard.

Ginnie: But what about your letter?

Richard: What letter?

Ginnie: To Mr Johnson. You said it was vital.

Richard: It *is* vital, it's about the new contract at the Royal Victoria Hall, we're opening up there on site in seven weeks ... send it off right away.

Ginnie: Well, you haven't finished it.

Richard: Well, how far have we got?

Ginnie: 'Dear Mr Johnson ... '

Richard is not destined to get far, for at that moment Eric, a newly appointed District Manager, comes in to see his boss. Richard is nonplussed, but welcoming as ever.

Richard: Ah, Eric, Eric, come in, come in. Sit down. Now, what can I do for you?

Eric: Well ... you asked me to pop in and see you.

Richard: Did we have an appointment? Sorry ... Why isn't it in the diary, Ginnie? Ah, it is. Oh yes, Monday's the day you start as District Manager, isn't it?

Eric: Yes, you said you'd brief me this afternoon.

Richard: Yes, of course. *Get* that flaming phone, would you Ginnie? I'm at a meeting.

Ginnie: It's the Managing Director's secretary. He's leaving his office and you said you had to talk to him this afternoon.

Richard: It can wait till tomorrow.

Ginnie: He's going abroad tomorrow for the week.

Richard: Tell him I'll catch him on the way down.

Ginnie: Hello – it's all right, he'll catch him on the way down – yes, like he usually does!

Richard: Ah well, Eric, there's nothing else I need tell you really. You're a good chap. You can handle it. Here are your car keys. Off you go!

Eric: But ... Mr Lewis.

Richard: Twelve contracts in your care. It's a big challenge. Good luck. Anything else you need to know, just ask Ginnie.

Ginnie: What about your call to Bernard?

Richard: Tell him I'll be down tomorrow.

Ginnie: And your letter to Mr Johnson?

Richard: Tomorrow!

Ginnie: But ...

Richard: Ginnie, I can't do *everything*!

Yes, a thoroughly conscientious character. And a dangerous one. Richard hasn't grasped *that it is easier to be busy than to get things done.* The result, of course, is that nobody surrounding him can get anything done either. His colleagues suffer, and so will his family. He'll never have enough time for them either, with the innumerable reports and memoranda he hasn't dealt with at the office transported nightly to his home. Those who have time for everybody end up

Organizing yourself

The problem with the unorganized manager is that in a sense he doesn't know he has a problem. Yes, he'll admit that life is chaotic from 9 a.m. to 5 p.m., that he takes a briefcase full of work home every night, that his reports are always late, that he occasionally – well, frequently – misses deadlines, that his life seems to be a constant stream of interruptions, that however fast he works he always seems to be behind, and that he is always having to busk his contributions at meetings because he's never had time to prepare. The unorganized manager will just accept that this is par for the course – the downside of having a responsible job, a reasonable salary and maybe the odd fringe benefit or two.

Being unorganized has a number of side-effects. These side-effects involve your staff. Chaos is contagious. Your staff won't be organized if you are not, because your lack of organization will be a constant source of disruption to them.

Similarly, your lack of organization will soon manifest itself to your boss and to your peers. They'll get the message that you are a busy chap but pretty soon will be asking themselves – busy at what?

Chaos is contagious.

with time for nobody. Of all this he is quite oblivious. In his own estimation he will, when he dies (prematurely, of course) be bound straight for the Celestial Executive Suite in the Sky where all Good Managers repose for eternity. Why not? He has tried his hardest. He deserves the best in after-life. But he will be in for a rude shock, and his reception will be exactly the opposite of what he expects.

Picture what happens. The inevitable coronary has occurred and he finds himself at the Gates of Heaven, confronted by St Peter …

St Peter: Hello. Can I help you?

Richard: Oh, pleased to meet you. What happens now?

St Peter: What did you have in mind?

Richard: Well … can I come in?

St Peter: Come *in*? I'll just check. Oh, sorry … I'm afraid you must be due at the other place.

Richard: But that's not possible. There must be a mistake. I've lived a good life … I've always made time for other people. I've always had an open door. I'm kind and patient, I've tried so hard to do things right, are you sure … ?

St Peter: You're on record as a classic

sinner, I'm sorry to say. A man who does evil while he thinks he's doing good.

Richard: Me? But I've always helped everyone. They all like me and appreciate what I've tried to do.

St Peter: You really think so? Would you like to see what one or two of them said about you only today?

So St Peter shows him a glimpse of life back on Earth. They listen to Ginnie ...

Ginnie: He's ghastly to work for. When he's in the office, I'm on edge all day. I never know what's happening or what to do and he'll never let me get on with my work. And when he's not messing me about I can never find him. He's always under pressure and snapping at me ...

And Eric ...

Eric: You just don't know where you are. When I really need his help, he never has time to talk about anything properly. I'm so confused about the job, and I've just got no confidence left ...

And Bernard ...

Bernard: And when you *do* get hold of him, he starts doing your job for you, checking everything and changing half of it just for the sake of it. He's absolutely hopeless.

And his wife Cathy ...

Cathy: I just hope he's not as appalling to work for as he is to live with – he forgets everything, even birthdays. Says he'll do things and cancels at the last

17

minute because he's never got time.
You can never rely on him ...

St Peter: See?
Richard: I don't believe it ... where did I
go wrong?

St Peter, of course, is right: as an ex-Pope
he is infallible. Richard is guilty of self-
delusion and doesn't realize that the
characteristics he most admires about himself are bad for business, bad for his family,
bad for his colleagues, bad for his company
and bad for himself. It isn't everybody who
gets a second chance, but St Peter is a
kindly soul, if that's the right word ...

Richard: Please – please give me one
more chance, *please.*
St Peter: Oh dear, I always dread this bit.
All right, but only if you promise to put
right all those things which you have
done wrong.
Richard: Fine. Er, what exactly?
St Peter: Well, where does one begin?
Allowing everyone else to interrupt you.
Doing jobs you don't need to do. Not
establishing your priorities ...
Richard: *Priorities?*
St Peter: Priorities. Misusing your
secretary, trying to do other people's
jobs for them. In other words, wasting
your own time and wasting everyone
else's.
Richard: I never.
St Peter: Yes you *did*! And you never
have enough time for your staff.
Richard: That's not true.
St Peter: Yes it is.
Richard: Well, I'm truly very sorry. But I
meant well. And I'll be a different
person if I can just have another
chance.
St Peter: You mustn't be a different

person. You must be the *same* person, *organized*.

Richard: I'll try. Thank you. You're an angel.

St Peter: No, just a saint.

Richard has been told a number of office truths – all of them new to him. He has been told to establish priorities, that he is supposed to be doing his own job and not other people's. That means, of course, that he has been introduced to the subtle concept of delegating, because if he isn't doing other people's jobs, then they have to do them. He has certainly grasped that he has to become more organized. Let's see how he handles his second chance ...

Ask yourself which is the more important, Mr Sidgewick – closing the Saudi deal, or designing a stretch cover for your sellotape dispenser ...

Richard: 'Morning Ginnie. Now let's make a really organized start today.

Ginnie: Mr Lewis, are you feeling all right? I heard you were taken ill last night.

Richard: Oh, yes, it was nothing, just a heart attack.

Establish your priorities.

Plan your time

Without planning, you'll never have the time for anything. Yes, initially, you may have to spend even more time to make time – but that is a sensible, positive investment. You have to take control of the time at your disposal and decide how you want to spend it. Time is a resource to be husbanded in the same way as you would treat raw materials or finished goods or stock in the business. Time also costs money. So if you have only a finite amount of time, and that time is expensive, it is crucial to plan out how it's going to be spent to most effect. This means clarifying the main purpose of your job.

Ask yourself: what am I here for? Those whose answers identify or match the purpose of the organization for which they work can award themselves several gold stars. Yes. Your purpose is to assist the organization in achieving its objectives, regardless of whether your job function is that of Data Processing Manager, Senior Welfare Officer, Sales Director or Typing Pool Supervisor. Being organized will help you to achieve those objectives. Having a plan is the first step on the way to that achievement.

Ginnie: Should you be here?

Richard: Yes, I'll be all right. Now, we've got all sorts of things to do today. We must make sure that we've got that marquee for Keith and I must write that letter to Mr Johnson and I want you to ring up Eric and see how he's getting on as District Manager – where's the post, by the way?

Ginnie: Here.

Richard: Ah, anything interesting?

Ginnie: I don't know, we haven't dealt with yesterday's yet.

Richard: Right, well let's do that now as well. Here's yesterday's – in fact, here's the whole pending tray. There's *weeks* of stuff here. Now I want you to take it all, go through it and chuck out anything we've missed the deadline for. Then summarize everything that's there, underlining anything that's vital. And *today's* post. And get Bernard on the phone for me right away … what's the matter?

Ginnie: When do you want it done by? In what order?

Richard: I want it all done now. Oh dear, don't be such a ninny, Ginnie. What's wrong now? *Stop crying!*

Not an outstanding success. To make progress, Richard will have to go right back to basics. He has to learn to plan, but also that *you can't learn how to plan if you don't know what to plan. He has to learn that doing your tasks is not the same thing as doing your job.* Above all, he has to know what *is* his own job. Could you describe yours accurately and succinctly? It is the key to planning. Fortunately, St Peter is on hand:

St Peter: You are the most unorganized person I know. Why don't you ever plan anything?

Richard: I do … Well, I haven't got time for planning.

St Peter: Without planning, you'll never have time for anything.

Richard: Look, I can't sit around planning what to do. I have got to get on and *do* it. I'm harassed, overworked and I haven't got the time – why do you think I had that coronary?

St Peter: As a matter of fact, we arranged that, to give your colleagues a bit of a break. Now stop panicking, sit down and listen. You must take control of your time and decide what you're going to spend it on. You must spend your time as carefully as you spend your money. It's a budget item. And an expensive one. Remember, you only have a finite amount of time – down there, anyway.

Richard: I see.

St Peter: Now. What are you down there for? What are you employed for?

Richard: Well, to check on my District Managers, do appraisals of subordinates and liaise with Finance.

St Peter: No, that's what you *do*. What is your purpose? Your purpose, you toy executive, is to provide quality food at prices your clients can afford while maximizing your profit margin. Am I correct?

Richard: Well, if you put it like that, yes. That is the company's purpose.

St Peter: Therefore it's yours. And to do it you need to control your time properly. Start by making a list of all the jobs you've got to get done.

Richard: What should be first?

St Peter: Write down everything, in any order. We'll sort them out later.

Richard: Right … well, let's see, there's Keith's marquee, my letter to Mr Johnson, the clients' trading accounts,

Make a 'to do' list

Make a list of all the jobs you have to get done, not just today's tray but your long-term tasks and priorities. It doesn't need to be in any order at this stage. Sorting it out comes later.

OK? Got your list? Now let's study its contents. It will doubtless be a mishmash of large and small tasks, the urgent and non-urgent, the immediate and the long-term, the boring and the interesting. Now start thinking about the items on your list and ensure that it also contains tasks which help you to achieve the *primary purpose of your job*.

Identifying active and reactive tasks

Tasks normally fall into two categories – active and reactive. The active positive tasks are the ones you must do to achieve the *objectives* of your job. The reactive tasks are all the junk that lands on your desk every day and has to be dealt with to keep things running. The danger, and this is the trap in which most unorganized managers are caught up, is that you will spend all the available time on reactive tasks – coping with the day-to-day jobs – and no time on the positive tasks.

So it is vital to be ruthless with yourself as you categorize your list and only allocate positive task status to those jobs which help you to build the business and achieve the objectives of the organization. The rest then become the reactive tasks – the daily running problems and maintenance needs.

organize the agricultural show, look at the new XG vending machine, renegotiate next year's contract with Bradley's, get tickets for the Health Safety and Hygiene Conference, sort out Bernard's problem ... My God, there's a hell of a lot to do. I'd better get on with it.

St Peter: *Not yet!* ... Now sort those tasks into two categories. The active positive tasks and the reactive tasks. It's all right, I'll explain. Always remember that the active positive tasks are the ones that help you to achieve the objectives of your job. The reactive tasks are all the junk that lands on your desk every day that you have to deal with to keep things running.

Richard: I see. Well – active positive tasks: organize the agricultural show, renegotiate next year's contract with Bradley's ...

St Peter: That's it. The active positive tasks are the ones that help you to build the business – to get more contracts and to make more profit on the ones you've already got. The reactive tasks, those are the everyday running problems. So sort those tasks into those two categories. Now, to plan your time properly, you must schedule each task properly.

Richard: *Schedule?*

St Peter: Yes, and before you schedule a task, you need to know two things about it. One, how long you want to spend on it, which is determined by how important it is. Two, how soon you need to get it done by, which is determined by how urgent it is. Importance and urgency are not the same thing. An urgent task is *not* necessarily important. It may be urgent but trivial – in which case do it straight away, but spend only a very few minutes on it, thereby leaving yourself lots of time for the important tasks. Positive active tasks are nearly always important. Reactive tasks are very often not important. So, judge the importance of each task by reference to that. *Then*, quite separately, deal with the matter of its urgency.

Richard: Supposing it's urgent and important?

St Peter: Then you deal with it straight away, and you give it a lot of time. It's not difficult! So when you sit down to schedule your time …

Richard: In my appointments diary?

St Peter: In your appointments diary … Block in big spaces of time for the important tasks – probably active positive ones – while leaving enough space for all the reactive ones that are going to land on your desk every day, a lot of which will be urgent but trivial. Goodbye.

Richard: … I'm not quite sure I've got it.

St Peter: All right, Ginnie will show you.

Richard: Ginnie!

St Peter: I shall personally inspire her. I haven't the time to train earthlings, I've got eternity to manage.

Priorities, scheduling his time, distinguishing between the urgent and the important, discovering that tasks can be active and necessarily reactive, learning that his job is what his company is about, not necessarily what he is actually doing, making plans to ensure that things get done in the right order … poor Richard! However, St Peter keeps his promise and so a divinely inspired Ginnie gets to work:

Richard: Any ideas, Ginnie?

Ginnie: Well, so we can leave lots of time

Schedule your work

You must start to schedule your work into the time you have available. To schedule a task you have to know two things:

1 How long you want to spend on the task.
   This is determined by how *important* that task is.
2 How soon you have to get the task completed.
   This is determined by how *urgent* the task is.

Importance and urgency are not the same thing. An urgent task is not necessarily important. It may be urgent but trivial. Deal with this sort of task straight away – don't spend all morning on it. In that way you'll leave yourself lots of time for the important tasks.

A good rule of thumb is to remember that the tasks on your list are nearly always the important ones. Reactive tasks are often not important. If you remember this, it will help you to sort out your schedules. If something is important and urgent, then it must take priority in your schedule.

Important positive tasks must be allocated sufficient time so that the work is completed within the prescribed deadline. Reactive tasks can then be slotted into the plan.

Your list and your schedule need updating daily. Priorities may change, there may be a shift in emphasis from cutting costs to increasing volumes. So each day your list needs to be updated and your schedule, where necessary, reorganized to cope with both the active and reactive tasks.

Using a secretary or managing without one

If you are lucky enough to have a secretary to yourself or have a 'share' in a secretary, then she can assist you in all

for important tasks, why don't we deal with reactive ones like normal people ... no offence ... first they open the letters, in the *morning*.

Richard: Do they?

Ginnie: Then they dictate replies immediately, or decide what action to take and actually take it, if you follow my meaning ... And they allow space for that in the appointments diary every morning.

Richard: Every morning? How long?

Ginnie: Half an hour?

Richard: That's a good idea. Half an hour every morning to react to the post. And then there's Eric. I must go out and see that he's doing all right, he's only just started as District Manager. So that takes care of this morning. Then I could pop back and see Bernard and drop in on a couple of sites – oh, and fix that light switch ...

Ginnie: Why not spend the whole day with Eric.

Richard: A whole day?

Ginnie: Yes. It's important, isn't it?

Richard: But what about my other Managers?

Ginnie: Give them each a whole day.

Richard: *Each* a whole day? But that's practically the whole week gone!

Ginnie: No. What about one next week and one the week after?

Richard: Next week. Yes. There's a week next week isn't there? That's true. That's an active task. I can schedule that in ahead of time. And I could leave some time free every day in case they wanted to talk to me in the meantime.

Ginnie: Great!

Richard: Oh that's fine, fine. OK, is that the diary done?

Ginnie: Well, didn't you want to see the Managing Director in his office?

Richard: Oh yes, you'd better fix up an appointment later.

Ginnie: Better do it now.

But it can't be done now. Again Keith, always sure of a welcome, bursts in.

Keith: Richard, got a minute?

Richard: Ah, Keith, yes, come in, come in, sit down.

Keith: Thanks. Gosh, what a terrible journey into work, traffic all the way, a great big articulated lorry had jackknifed and caused a two-mile jam. There was …

Then Richard hears a Voice …

St Peter: Is this important? Essential for your work?

And responds sharply:

Richard: Keith, do you really mean a minute?

Keith: Eh?

Richard: I have got a *minute*, but if you want longer we'll have to do it later.

Keith: Oh well, no, not really, I just wanted to know about my marquee.

Richard: I'm chasing that up this morning. Anything else? No? Good. That's fine, lovely, well look it's been very nice to see you.

Keith: Have I … upset you in some way old chap?

Richard: No.

Ginnie: Wednesday afternoon?

Richard: Ah yes, I'm keeping Wednesday afternoons free, you know, in case things crop up. You could drop in then.

Keith: Oh. Great. Fine. See you then.

Exit Keith.

this. That is, of course, providing you tell her what it is you're up to.

By understanding your priorities, she can assist you in achieving them. This will also make her realize the positive tasks in her own job. Schedule morning dictation sessions and diary update sessions. Ensure that if she has to type up a report for one of your positive tasks, the schedule in the diary allows her time to do it, you time to check it and edit it, and further retyping if required. Agree with her some free times – no appointments – for either catching up or thinking. In other words, get her to see your time as a resource which she must husband wisely too.

For those without a secretary: *Nil Desperandum*, but you'll just have to be ruthless with yourself on occasions. If you have a report to write or figures to prepare or a complex problem to think through, then your office or work area may not always be the most suitable venue for this activity. Is there a meeting room you can borrow, or a spare office, or would your organization allow you to go to the local library or even to work at home whilst completing this task? This venue business should be resolved as you schedule the task in your diary – you block out the time and simultaneously enter where you will be working. On occasions you may need to get your telephone calls redirected or messages taken by the switchboard.

Use your diary

The diary is one of the primary instruments of management and the organized manager knows how to use it. He schedules chunks of time in the diary so that he can achieve his positive tasks. So time will be set aside for preparing and writing reports, visiting major clients and potential clients, for trips to major installations. Having done this, the organized manager can then take time to cope with the daily round, because he's an organized person who knows that too many appointments or meetings in one day will wreck his time plan and that meetings shouldn't be placed back-to-back in the diary; there needs to be a breathing space in between. This breathing space can be used to catch up with a reactive task – an urgent phone call, some rapid dictation arising from the previous meeting or even to cope with a small time overrun from the previous meeting. The organized manager also schedules time to 'walk the job', to visit his departments and to talk to the staff. It is an important task – after all, it is the staff who help the organized manager achieve his objectives.

Richard: Well done, Ginnie.

Ginnie: Shall I put your available time in the appointments diary then, and notify everyone?

Richard: Notify them?

Ginnie: Tell them that's when you're available to see them – so they realize when you're *not*.

Richard: Realize when I'm not available? Oh happiness! Oh, Ginnie, you're a tower of strength. Now then, let me see, just a minute, there's nothing down there for Thursday. *It's completely wasted.*

Ginnie: That's your time for long-term discussion, to improve next year's profits.

Richard: What discussion?

Ginnie: Where we're going, future plans. And I've allowed fifteen minutes at the end of each day to coordinate the diaries and make out tomorrow's list. And I've got bring forward files, a wall chart and a year planner.

Richard: What for?

Ginnie: Long-term scheduling. For your regular meetings. So you don't have to remember anything, and you can see things at a glance.

It's that Voice again.

St Peter: So what do you do after you've made your list and established your priorities?

Richard: I schedule my time in my appointments diary.

St Peter: And how do you divide it up?

Richard: I schedule the positive active tasks – the things I'm here for – leaving time for the reactive tasks – the problems that crop up from day to day.

St Peter: *Now* you have organized yourself! Hallelujah!

Ginnie has opened a new world for Richard – a world of properly kept diaries, 'to do' lists, 'bring forward' files and visual planners. Let's look at these in more detail.

The diary should not be a repository of 'reactive' appointments and dates. Constructively used, it should be a tool for the future in which time for planning, time for your own availability for others – and of course non-availability – the scheduling of important tasks which need time to be set aside for them, regular meetings with colleagues which could well go by default through simply not ensuring that they happen, etc. etc., are enshrined.

A 'to do' list isn't a mere jumble of immediate problems. It should be a guide in itself to those tasks which are active and reactive, important and trivial, urgent and not urgent. Some of the most important tasks – the active ones concerned with your real job – will sit on that list for weeks, provided that the requisite time is laid aside for actually accomplishing them in an effective manner.

Bring Forward files can be like a second memory – almost certainly better than your first! A regular reminder of tasks which are 'pending' (probably they will be pending because they require something else to happen before you can deal with them) can be an essential piece of office equipment.

Visual planners accurately and regularly updated can save hours of leafing through ill-assorted figures and reports. Whether they are used for production schedules, staff holidays or whatever, once they are at work they will be working for you.

Finally, Ginnie has introduced to Richard a proper use of his secretary. She knows her job and wants to be left to get on with it; she also wants to help him do his, but has had to wait until he knows what his job is before she

Use bring forward files

A bring forward file is like acquiring a second memory. It's extremely useful for keeping abreast of the reactive tasks and for prompting you to start preparing and collecting data for your positive tasks. Need an answer to your query by Friday? Drop a reminder in the bring forward file. Expecting a price from a supplier next month? Put a chasing note in the month file in case you don't hear.

Use visual planners

Why search through a mountain of paper when a simple bar or line chart, which is updated weekly or monthly, can demonstrate sales figures, costs, work in progress, despatch volumes or whatever data you need to help keep you abreast of what is going on? The chart can show you comparisons with previous years and once set up it becomes an active document, quick to update and simple to assimilate.

Similarly, various types of year planners can help to schedule staff holidays, training activities, exhibitions, specialist promotions, sales cycles, etc. This same information on separate documents in separate files doesn't give you a complete picture and also takes hours to sort out. When the information is merged, presented visually and updated regularly, it can alert you to potential crises and point out planning gaps, etc.

How to delegate

To delegate or not to delegate is the quandary most managers face. Delegation can be a risky business but the risks only occur if the delegation process is not handled properly. With proper planning and training, a manager can minimize the risk involved.

First of all you have to get over the following feelings:

1 Fear of losing control.
2 Regret at giving up jobs you enjoy.
3 Belief that you can cope with the job yourself.

Some management and organizational structure gurus say that managers need at least four or five subordinates. Why? Because an energetic,

can be properly confident in her own. Hallelujah indeed.

But having learned how to arrange himself, is John fully equipped to organize other people? He now has to get to grips with the true art of delegating and to learn that *delegating is not a convenient device for continuing to interfere.*

Bernard: So what do you think: minestrone or chicken soup? A choice of two main dishes or three? And do you want *me* to advertise for the new kitchen porter?
Richard: That's up to you.
Bernard: Yes, but as you always change my decisions, I thought I'd ask you first. *That* way, you can change them before I've made them, if you follow me.
Richard: I only do your work because you can't even breathe in and out without asking me how to do it.
Bernard: Yes, well, you keep interfering, you keep delegating jobs to me and then taking them back. I can never discuss anything with you and then you blow me up when it goes wrong.
Richard: Aagh!

Richard consults St Peter:

Richard: He's made me ill again.
St Peter: You've made yourself ill again. Bernard's absolutely right. And if you don't pull your socks up, I'm going to recall you to the after-life on a permanent basis. You've learned to organize yourself. Now learn to organize other people. You must learn to delegate.
Richard: But I *do* delegate. I left Ginnie to manage my bring forward files.
St Peter: It's her job anyway, that's secretarial work. I'm talking about you

delegating part of your job.

Richard: Part of *my* job?

St Peter: Well, that's what delegation is, isn't it? Giving your subordinates the authority to decide, and without consulting you. Now, there are two barriers you've to get through. The first one is that you have to give up doing some jobs that you like doing. There's a technical phrase for this: it's called growing up. Then you have to get over your fear of losing control.

Richard: But if my subordinates get it wrong, then I'll have to take the rap.

St Peter: Of course. Because it's part of *your* job you've delegated. You can delegate tasks and authority – you cannot delegate accountability.

Richard: It's still my job, although someone else is doing it?

St Peter: Yes. Your boss gets blamed for your mistakes and praised for your successes ...

Richard: Well?

St Peter: So he'll understand if your subordinates make a few mistakes when work is first delegated to them, but he'll be pleased that you've delegated it because that'll mean you'll have more time for more important things.

Richard: It's such a risk.

St Peter: Of course it is, but with proper planning and training you can *limit* the risk. Now first of all get it clear in your mind which task to delegate. Then ask yourself who is the person who can handle it, and then how long will it take him or her to learn to handle it. You can't delegate a new job without proper training. It's not fair on them and it'll only involve you in more work later on. It takes time for a person to learn and to gain confidence. You've got to teach them, and you've got to make a training

organized manager can usually cope with more than one job for a while. But, these gurus say, given five or more subordinates, a manager can't do all their work, therefore he will be forced:

1 To delegate.
2 Not to interfere.

So watch out if you head a team of two or three people – you'll have to discipline yourself about delegation. Also remember that the positive tasks for your subordinates are not going to be your positive tasks. So, if you interfere in their activities you won't have the right amount of time to devote to your own priorities. And you won't lose control if you delegate properly. In fact the reverse will take place – you'll gain overall control. If you don't delegate, you'll pretty soon get bogged down in too much detail. As a manager, you should be in overall control of the action.

The fact that you are not intimately involved in analyzing data is not important. What is important is that you ensure that the analysis, if required, is carried out and you know when and where the data is available.

Yes, you will have to carry the can for your team if mistakes take place – in the same way as your boss is accountable for the mistakes you make. On the positive side, you bathe in the reflected glory of your team's achievements. The chances are that these achievements will be many if you are organized and delegate

Delegation is not the same as abdication.

effectively.

No, delegation isn't about dumping the rubbish, finding some convenient dustbin person to whom to give all the jobs you hate or find boring. Delegating does not mean giving someone a task to perform: it means giving them a result to achieve. Delegation is about passing across part of your job – giving your subordinates the authority to decide, without consulting you, and giving them responsibility while you retain overall accountability – the carrying of the can.

So what you need to do is:

1 Decide which task to delegate.
2 Decide to whom you will delegate it.
3 Brief and train the individual.
4 Inform other people about the change.

The problem with most managers is they can't let go. They are like the amateur car mechanic who won't leave well alone and who is permanently

plan so that they know exactly when they're going to have to take full responsibility for the job. For example, what about that wretched letter to Mr Johnson?

Richard: Yes. I've got to do something about that. We open up at the Royal Victoria Hall in seven weeks.

St Peter: Well don't try to do it yourself. Delegate it to the District Manager.

Richard: Bernard?

St Peter: Well, why not? That's what he's there for.

Richard: What if it goes wrong?

St Peter: Look, there's nothing to worry about provided that you delegate it properly, provided that you …

Richard, all enthusiasm for this delegating business, has rushed back to Earth. It was, unquestionably, a good idea to delegate the job to Bernard, but it would have been even better if Richard had stayed long enough to hear what St Peter was going to say next. *Delegation is not the same thing as abdication* and Richard is about to make an elementary mistake …

Richard: Bernard, I've got a proposal for

you. I want *you* to take over the Royal Victoria Hall job.

Bernard: How do you mean?

Richard: I'm delegating it to you. All of it. I'm putting you in charge. Just you.

Bernard: Me?

Richard: How can I make it any clearer? Organize the staff, buy light equipment – cutlery, crockery, whisks, the usual – set out all the documentation and bookwork, organize the notices, health and safety, training, our policy statement – and make sure that they're adhered to. Any questions?

Bernard: But all this stuff you're handing over to me – you've never allowed me to do it before.

Richard: I know, that's been my mistake. I'm asking you to do it and you know how, don't you? Fine. Now it's all up to you. I want you to stand on your own feet – I don't want to hear another word about it until I see you there on the opening day. It's all yours, mate!

Inevitably, Richard is summoned back by St Peter.

Richard: What am I doing here now? Why don't you let me get on with it?

St Peter: Because there's something else you have to learn.

Richard: I decided which task, who did it, and by when they'd be ready. He doesn't need any more help or training, he's already trained, so he's ready, right? And I briefed him.

St Peter: Yes, but …

Richard: Shut up! I informed others. I got it *all* right. So what have you got me up here again for? I can't spend time hanging around in Heaven when I've got important things to do down there.

tinkering with the engine. For most managers the natural tendency is to interfere with their subordinates' work, to double-check everything, to override decisions and to change things behind the subordinate's back. This is not done in a malicious way but usually stems from a misguided sense of helping the subordinate or trying to ensure that the job goes correctly. And if you're always happy to take the job back or to check everything, then your subordinates will let you.

What you need to do is to set up a series of systems or meetings to monitor the progress of the task once you have delegated it. The methods of monitoring should be agreed with the person to whom the job has been delegated. As the person's confidence grows, and as they gain more experience with the passage of time, these checks and meetings can be less frequent. Always remember:

1 Be available for advice.
2 Actively check up on key points.

St Peter: Would you care to look into the future?

Richard looks – apprehensively ...

Richard: Ah, Bernard, come on in, come and sit down. Well now, how's it all going at the Victoria Hall?
Bernard: OK. But I think you ought to know that as you left it to me, I've played safe.
Richard: How do you mean, played safe?
Bernard: Well, the unions wanted a special deal for overtime.
Richard: Why didn't you tell me?
Bernard: You didn't ask. You said it was up to me. So I thought ... I'll have to give them what they're asking for.
Richard: My God. Is *this* the budget? It's a certain loss-maker. I could get the sack for this.
Bernard: You said you didn't want to be bothered.
Richard: But ... but ...

Richard demands an explanation from St Peter.

Richard: But I delegated it to Bernard. I gave him the job and left him to do it.
St Peter: Well, you gave him the authority to do the job, yes, but that doesn't mean you can just walk away from it.
Richard: You're confusing me. Leave him alone to do the job, but don't just walk away.
St Peter: Let's find an everyday example. Take your son, Darren.
Richard: Darren?
St Peter: Yes, Darren. Now, when you taught him to swim, you didn't just go home and leave him to it, did you? You got out of the pool, sure, but kept an eye on him in case of trouble, and as he

became a stronger swimmer, so you needed to watch him less. Well, it's the same with delegation. You take your hands off but you keep your eyes open. So, be available to give advice in case you are needed, and monitor progress, check up on key points.

And it works. Bernard did not, actually, commit himself …

Bernard: … But then I thought I'd better check with you.
Richard: You mean – it's not too late?
Bernard: No.
Richard: Oh, Bernard. Thank you, thank you, thank you, thank you …

So Richard has realized that one of the essential components in delegating is a proper degree of continued involvement. Of course you follow Heavenly principles: make sure you know exactly what it is you are delegating, to whom the tasks are going, that they are capable of handling them, and that all people concerned should know who is now doing that particular job. But it is absolutely essential to remember that the person who delegates a task cannot simply wash his hands of it. It is a balance which the good manager, like the good parent, will get right. Once you get it right, you will come home in the evenings and cope as easily as Richard does now!

Richard, at last with time for his family, has succeeded in mending his son's toy train.

Darren: Daddy, it's super!
Richard: Well, you go and get your face scrubbed. We're going to the pictures.
Darren: Great!
Cathy: What about your work?
Richard: Work? Oh … *work*. I do that at the office now.

Golden rules

If you cannot manage yourself, you cannot manage anyone.

You cannot know *how* to plan if you don't know *what* to plan.

The manager who doesn't know *his* job ensures that nobody else knows theirs.

Those who have time for everyone end up having time for no one.

It is easier to be busy than to get things done.

What is urgent is not necessarily the same as what is important.

Doing your tasks is not the same as doing your job.

Delegation is not to be confused with abdication.

Delegation is not about giving tasks to perform; it is about giving a result to achieve.

Time is a budget item, and an expensive one at that.

2 Decisions, decisions

Making decisions is one of the basic tasks of management, but it is also an area where a great deal of trouble often starts. This is not just because the decision may be a wrong one; there can be plenty of problems even with the correct ones. You, as a manager, may quite easily come to a decision in the privacy of your office. It is possible, however, that you are not the right person to be taking the decision at all. And if you are, have you given yourself every chance to ensure that it is the best one you can make – even that the decision to make a decision was right? And, suppose you have – then what? You have to make sure that something happens. How do you set about that, and have you taken all practical steps to see that what happens is properly implemented – and that there are no unforeseen snags along the way?

One obvious problem lies not in taking the decision itself but in communicating it to those who are affected. 'Why didn't they ask me?' or, 'I could have told them it wouldn't work,' or even, 'We were not consulted, we refuse to cooperate with the decision' are common complaints. You may be thinking: 'But I don't take that kind of earth-shattering decision' – which is not the point. Virtually *all* decisions affect others, and if they are badly handled without sufficient fore-thought, consultation, follow-up, etc., the consequences can be considerable.

Of course, not all decisions are equally important, or of the same type. Broadly, your decisions will fall into three categories. First, the emergency decisions which require clear, quick and precise action in a crisis. Second, the routine decisions of an everyday nature (approving a petty cash slip or agreeing to a minor change in a shift rota) – pretty simple, but never allow 'routine' to be a synonym for 'thoughtless'. Third, there are the debatable decisions, those which will involve changes and, needless to say, these are the decisions which demand the most time and the most preparation. Here are five vital stages which should be part of all such decisions:

1 Fact gathering.
2 Consultation.
3 Taking the decision.
4 Communicating the decision.
5 Following up.

Do all managers follow these principles? Let's examine them in more detail, following the experiences of a particular manager, Alan Robinson, who was given the job of moving his company into a new office building. Everything has gone wrong. He is sitting in his office, alone and depressed, wondering what caused so many mistakes. Surely other people have had more difficult problems to cope with. How did *they* manage … ? Suddenly, as if in a dream, he finds himself before an examination board of four of history's great decision-takers: Field-Marshal Montgomery, Queen Elizabeth I, Winston Churchill and the man who organized the assassination of Caesar, Brutus. They take him, backwards in time, through the various stages of the office move and show him how he ignored or neglected all the basic principles of good decision-making. They also show him how their own great moments of decision would have worked out if Alan had been in their shoes …

Monty: What's the matter, man? Haven't you been in front of a review panel before? Now, tonight we're going to teach you a thing or two about how to take decisions.
Churchill: And how to get commitment to them.
Elizabeth: No good making a decision if thou canst not get it executed.
Brutus: Thus so.

Monty: Now, as I understand it, you're an ordinary, reasonably efficient young manager who got put in charge of the office move.

Alan: Yes, that's right.

Monty: Tell us about it.

Alan: Well, it began like this ...

The scene shifts to that happy day when an exuberant Alan rushed in to show Mary, his secretary, the new plans.

Alan: Mary, the new offices are terrific! It's a smashing building. They'll be perfect.

Mary: Have you just been there?

Alan: No, I've been with the architects. But I've got all the plans here.

Mary: You mean you haven't actually seen it?

Alan: Oh yes, on Friday night. Only a quick look. I was a bit pushed. But it's all in the plans. Fine.

Mary: Lots of room?

Alan: Lots. Means we can get the Design Department in too.

Mary: I didn't realize you'd got stuck with it. I thought you just had to make suggestions.

Alan: No. I've got to decide when we move, who goes where, which department goes first. The whole thing, I think. Yes, me and the Planning Manager. Well, you know, he understands these things. I mean he is a planner. We're doing it together, but I'm sort of doing most of it. See, I've worked out who goes in what part of the building.

Mary: Sales on the third floor?

Alan: Yes, next to the bar and restaurant, they'll like that. Accounts on the fourth, with Design, Production on the fifth and P.R. on the sixth.

Decide what you are deciding

When you have to make a decision, it is all too easy to overlook several important points. For example, is it your decision alone? Establish clearly the limits of your responsibility. What is your decision supposed to achieve? What are the limiting factors? (E.g. is cash a problem? Is overtime possible?) What are you really deciding about? A decision seems necessary on the X project, but is it really? Would tackling a bigger issue actually resolve the decision on the X project anyway?

Mary: When are we moving?

Alan: Christmas. It's a pretty slack time for us.

Mary: But Alan, aren't Sales very busy then?

Alan: Oh yes, but moving doesn't affect Sales much, does it? They're hardly here. Nothing like the rest of us.

Mary: It must have taken you ages to work out the plans.

Alan: Yes, the whole weekend. I'll just ring the M.D. and tell him about it … Ah, hello sir. We've worked everything out. I've managed to get the Design Department in and I've given the architect the go-ahead on the floor. Er … yes … I'm sorry, sir. No, I'll call him straight away. I'm sorry …

Mary: What is it?

Alan: He doesn't want Design moved. He says the Board never … Oh, forget it. Hours of work, that was.

Right from the beginning Alan has not distinguished himself. He *thought* he knew the scope of his responsibility, but failed to clear a fairly simple point with the Managing Director. There is obvious confusion about who is actually in charge of what, and some important preliminary work has not been done, ensuring that the work actually done has to be done again. Montgomery can spot a poor bit of staff-work and sums up succinctly:

Monty: You hadn't collected the facts. You weren't crystal clear in your mind what decisions had to be made, and which ones you were in charge of. And then you didn't ask yourself what information you needed.

Alan: I did. I knew …

Monty: Did you ask Sales or Accounts or Production exactly what their requirements were?

Alan: I thought I knew.

Monty: And were you right?

Alan: Well, I did speak to the architect and the Planning Manager. I looked at the plans ...

Monty: You can't tell everything from plans. You've got to get off your backside and go out and look for yourself. Do a reconnaissance. Imagine if you'd been running my battles!

Another minute and your soufflés will be ruined ...!

Establish the limits of your responsibility.

Alan is forced to watch himself in Monty's place addressing officers and his generals ...

Alan: Right, now here's what has been decided. At twenty-two hundred hours, the Fifth and Sixth Armoured Divisions will move through here, across the plain and make a big push here and here.

A General: Who's in charge of the operation, sir?

Alan: I am, I think. Me or Alexander. Or Patten. One of us. I'll find out.

General: About the terrain, sir, is it hard or soft?

Alan: The map doesn't say.

General: What's the weather been like?

Alan: Oh dreadful, hasn't it.

39

Know the facts

The first part of fact-finding is knowing what you are doing and where you are going. The second part is knowing where to find the facts. Obviously, depending on the type of problem or project you are looking at, different sources of information will apply. Some of the following sources may act as a checklist for you:

1 Company procedures manuals
2 Job descriptions
3 Standards of performance – actuals and agreed levels

General: No, *there* sir.
Alan: There? … Er … well …
General: Have the tank commanders got enough fuel, sir?
Alan: I expect so. They'd have said if they hadn't, wouldn't they?
General: Won't they need air support?
Alan: They'd better not. I spent the weekend working this one out.
General: It's Mr Churchill on the phone, sir. He wants to know why you're attacking the French.
Alan: Hello? Yes, I know they're our allies, sir, but that's exactly what'll give us the vital element of surprise … Stick to the Germans, right. But you did say 'big attack', you know. I mean, I put in a lot of hours on this plan.

Monty turns a withering eye to Alan.

Monty: See what I mean?
Alan: That's not fair. That's not what I was doing.
Monty: It's exactly what you were doing. You can't make proper decisions until you collect the facts. First, clarify which decisions are yours. Second, decide what information you need. Third, go out and get it.

Monty has given a crucial checklist. Of course, Alan will have to think hard about *how* to follow it. But good managers will certainly not make a decision without knowing what decisions are within their responsibility and they won't take them without knowing the facts on which to base that decision. They will also have mastered where to get those facts. For example, in many cases, somebody inside or even outside the company will have direct experience of similar decisions. *Never be afraid to draw on the experience of others*. Nobody should want to overburden themselves with useless information, but once you know exactly what you are doing, and therefore what is relevant to your particular decision, *you cannot be too well informed*. So, once you are equipped, what then? Over to the Great Decision-Makers:

Monty: Now, once I knew what decisions were mine and what information I needed, and after I'd gone out and got it, then I could move on to the next stage.

Alan: Giving orders?

Elizabeth: No, thou nincompoop, CONSULTATION. Thou hast heard of consultation?

Alan: Yes, Your Highness. I just didn't think Generals did much of it.

Elizabeth: Of course they do, thou mooncalf. *Queens* consult. How else dost thou imagine a mere woman defeated the Spanish? By reading *Teach Thyself to Thrash Armadas*? Thou must consult those underlings affected by thy decision. Didst thou?

Alan: A bit …

Once again a scene from Alan's past is flashed before him:

Alan: Well now, I've called this meeting because, as you know, I've been put in charge of the move and I wanted to consult all the section heads about it. Now I've drawn up these plans.

John Barton, Head of Accounts, bursts angrily into the room.

Barton: What's going on?

Alan: Ah, John, I wondered where you were.

Barton: What's all this about my department moving?

4 Sales figures – budgets and actuals
5 Computer data
6 Union agreements
7 Personnel files
8 Company library
9 Central filing
10 Press cuttings on the company and its competitors
11 Chairman's statements
12 Internally held stock exchange reports on the company
13 Staff selection/retention data
14 Old files – probably removed to a dead files store
15 Long-service employees
16 Old company annual reports and accounts
17 Company house journals
18 Maintenance reports
19 Shift books
20 Absence and labour turnover statistics
21 Debtors lists

Some of these, and many other sources, will exist within your organization. Then think what the outside world might have to offer. Have other companies trodden a similar path before you? Will they swap information with you? Is there a trade organization that can help? Is there an institute which has validated the techniques or equipment you are investigating? What competitive products are available other than the plant on offer to you? Who else has the equipment or service on offer? What are their experiences?

Alan: Well, I told you, didn't I?

Barton: You did not.

Alan: I'm sorry, I thought I had, sorry.
Look, sit down. Now's the chance for
us all to discuss it.

Barton: When's it to be? Three weeks?

Alan: Well, we're not actually discussing
the timing of the move today, because
that hasn't been worked out yet. But
what we're discussing today is who goes
where in the new building. Okay? I'd
like your views. This is what I've
decided, sorry, worked out. The Sales
Department will be a bit smaller
because it's on the third floor, but
that's, well, because the sales people are
out a lot. Oh, incidentally, the bar and
restaurant are on the third floor too, so
that'll be nice, won't it? Now,
unfortunately there may have to be a bit
of sharing of desks. Still, you've all got
your own company cars, haven't you? So
you can't complain. You know, swings
and roundabouts. One drawback is that
there isn't any room for your secretaries
on the third floor, but we can move
them up to the fifth floor, to the typing
pool ...

McDonald, the Sales Manager, has something to say ...

McDonald: Who the hell do you think
you are?

Alan: What?

McDonald: How dare you? We need
company cars to do our work, so as to
keep people like you in jobs. And what's
all this about sharing desks? Are *you*
going to be sharing a desk?

Alan: Er, no ...

McDonald: Let's get one or two things
perfectly clear before we go any further,
shall we? My salesmen do not prop up

bars, except when they have to go away on long, boring trips on company business. They do *not* share desks and they *will* have their secretaries in their offices. All right?

Alan: They can't. There isn't any more room on the third floor.

McDonald: Then I'm not having the third floor.

Alan: You've got to. The Board has approved this plan.

McDonald: And how are you going to make me?

Deadlock. Lack of consultation has led to confrontation. Alan has broken every rule: McDonald may have a good case for not moving to the third floor, but Alan hasn't even troubled to find out. He may have a bad case, but Alan has not given him the chance to agree to move with a sensible discussion about the merits and demerits of the position. Moreover, by presenting his views so insensitively, he has made certain that the pros and cons don't come into it at all. By seeming to walk over the legitimate considerations of colleagues, he has walked instead into a hole of his own making. *Never spring a surprise you don't have to.* Even if you can't see a problem, others might. Queen Elizabeth, who had to unite such diverse and eminent characters as Drake, Hawkins, Walsingham and Burghley at a supreme moment of crisis in national history, spells it out in words of more than one syllable:

Queen Elizabeth: Consider this well. Consultation is a process factual and a process psychological.

Alan: Come again?

Queen Elizabeth: Oh, stone the dagoes. Can't you manage anything over two syllables? All right, modern English. There's two dead good reasons for

Involve other people

Nothing demotivates people more than the frustration of not being asked or involved in the decisions that affect them. Over a period of time this makes them antagonistic to *any* new plans. The time and energy wasted in repairing the damage caused by lack of consultation and involvement is far greater and less fruitful than spending time thoughtfully at an earlier stage.

consulting people, baby. The first is to see if there are any facts you've missed or got wrong. You nearly always find there's something important you hadn't grasped. Right? That's the first reason. The second is psychological. When you make your decision, some people may not like it, but you want them to carry it out with reasonable enthusiasm and without being obstructive about it. Well, before you decide, ask their opinion and *listen* to it! If people feel they've at least had the chance to influence your decision, they're going to feel much more involved and committed to it than if it is taken over their heads. I can imagine you in my shoes in 1588 ...

Alan is in charge of the Armada.

Alan: Gentlemen, the Armada. I have decided we shall attack it in the Bay of Biscay.
Drake: Your Majesty!
Alan: Yes, Drake?
Drake: If we can assail them in the English Channel we can outmanoeuvre them and replenish our ships each day, Your Majesty.
Alan: Now, who's Queen around here?
Burghley: But surely you wish to hear your Council's advice, Your Majesty?
Alan: I spent the weekend on this, Burghley.
Walsingham: Yes, but Your Majesty ...
Alan: Walsingham, are you disputing my decision?
Drake: Look, we *are* the sailors ...
Alan: And I'm the bloody Queen. You'll do your job and I'll do mine. Now, go on, all of you, off to Biscay. What's the problem?
Hawkins: Er ... I've got a migraine.
Drake: And I've got a bowls match.

Walsingham: My grandmother's dying.
Alan: You take a decision and they all get bloody-minded.

Consultation means 'to seek information or advice from and to take into consideration the feelings and interests of others'. Assuming that you are taking decisions that affect your team, it seems logical to consult them before deciding. *Before* is vital. This is not a process of asking for a blessing on a decision that has already been taken. You need to listen to what your team has to say. You cannot possibly be in possession of all the

Communicate your decision to those affected.

facts or have all of the ideas on what to do. The more brains the better. This is not consensus. You are not asking them to agree or take a majority vote on what should be done. This is a process of posing the problem and asking them how they suggest it could be resolved. It is unlikely that you will be taking the decision on the spot. Therefore, you can go away to think about the ideas and information they put forward. Above all you will have given yourself the chance to consider your *options*. A precipitate decision, before you have gathered the facts, before you have properly consulted, and before you have weighed up the results of those consultations and any alternatives which may emerge, is rank bad management.

Remember also to consult those on the fringe of the decision. Managers often go to enormous pains to consult their direct staff but forget to consult employees who will be indirectly affected by a decision. For instance, if a new computer form for orders is required, in many cases the computer staff and the administration people will be consulted. But what about the poor salesman out in the field? He may well be the last to be told, long after the design decision has been taken, even though he is the one who is going to have to fill in the form.

Alan can see all this when it's pointed out, but he still has a problem:

Alan: I can see that the right decision is usually clear if you've prepared for it properly. But supposing it isn't. Supposing you've considered and consulted and gathered your options, and you still don't know what is right, what do you do then?

Monty: Toss a coin! If your decision is so marginal that you still can't decide, decide arbitrarily. But remember, if it comes down heads, be committed to heads.

Alan: Are you serious?

Monty: Serious and right. Once you've decided, you must give a commitment to your decision, otherwise you can't sell it to your chaps. Right, Prime Minister?

Churchill: I agree. And the next step is, communicate your decision. Make sure everyone knows what it is. Persuade them that it's right.

Alan: Persuade them?

Churchill: That never occurred to you,

The marginal decision

Sometimes, of course, the right decision is not obvious. So how, then, do you make up your mind?

The following points may help:

1 Remind yourself of the objective.

did it? You must be prepared to persuade others to follow your decision. Now, how did you actually tell them about your office move?

Alan: I just told them …

The scene shifts to moving day, and the results of Alan's idea of what constitutes telling …

Removal Man: This is the Accounts Department, right?

Barton: Yes.

Removal Man: Right. I'm moving you today.

Barton: Wrong. A week today. The Production Department moves today.

Removal Man: No. That's a week today.

Barton: In that case, how do you account for the fact that they are all packed up, sitting there waiting to go?

Removal Man: I can't help that. My orders are to move you now.

Alan: What's the trouble?

Barton: This gentleman insists on moving us today, when we are not ready to move and Production are.

Alan: Well, why aren't you ready?

Barton: Because we're not supposed to be until next week.

Alan: Who told you that?

Barton: You did.

Alan: I didn't. I know precisely what I told you.

Barton: Well, apparently you don't. Anyway, he can't move us. Look what he's brought, tea chests!

Removal Man: What's wrong with tea chests?

Barton: You can't put all this expensive equipment into tea chests! We need specialists, someone who knows how to move computers, not wardrobes.

2 Reassess the priorities.
3 Consider the options – giving equal weight to those in accordance with your own prejudices and those not.
4 Indulge in some lateral thinking – are there any other options not yet considered or suggested?
5 Put pros/cons against each option.
6 Choose whichever option best meets the objectives and priorities of the situation.

Remember the 'least worst' rule: if there is no perfect solution, you may have to accept the best of a bad bunch. Before making up your mind you may have to 'sleep' on the facts. In other words, follow points one to five as above, but give your brain a chance to sort them out overnight before taking a decision the following morning.

Timing is vital. It's no good spending all your time researching and consulting your people so that you have no time to consider the information gathered. Fix a schedule which allows you time to decide. After considering all the hard-earned facts and opinions which you have gathered, you may realize that a decision of 'no decision' is necessary. This may require considerable courage from you, as by now a number of people will have been built up to anticipate a change. However, if it is the 'least worst' decision, this is the one you should follow.

Brief in a group

How you communicate the decision, and to whom, is critical. Too often managers tell people about decisions in a random fashion. Assuming you have consulted people, it is vital that you brief them as a group, once the decision is made. Telling individuals on an *ad hoc* basis plays straight into the hands of the rumour-mongers and will probably mean a considerable amount of chat on the grapevine.

It is vital, therefore, that you brief the team collectively. At this briefing you should go through the following:

1 What you have decided.
2 When the decision will take effect.
3 Where the changes will take place.
4 How the decision will be implemented.
5 Who will be affected.
6 Why you have chosen this way of solving the situation.

Although you may not be the world's greatest orator, it is vital that when you communicate the 'why' you use all your skills of persuasion and outline the benefits. Your job is to 'sell' your decisions.

Churchill glares at Alan.

Churchill: So, that was your idea of a briefing was it? Nobody knew what was said or to whom. Always brief in a group. You've got to give them the opportunity of asking questions. And you've got to make sure that everybody understands what you've said to everyone else. Imagine this in 1944, I can just see you in charge of D Day …

WRAC: The Chief of Air Staff would like to see you immediately, sir.
Alan: I'm busy.
WRAC: He's heard a rumour from the Admiralty that D-Day is tomorrow.
Alan: A rumour? It *is* tomorrow!
WRAC: Does General Eisenhower know, sir?
Alan: Of course he knows. I had dinner with him on Monday. Don't the services ever get together? This is chaotic …

Churchill emphasizes his point.

Churchill: When you have briefed people together, always back up your briefing in writing. People's memories are not perfect. So …
Alan: Communicate your decision.
Churchill: Exactly. Always brief people together. Be prepared to sell your decision. Then, confirm it in writing.
Monty: Right-ho. After communicating your decision, what then?
Alan: Well, one hopes that it's acted upon.
Monty: Does one do more than *hope*? Does one check, for instance?
Alan: Of course. It's common sense.

Common sense maybe. But giving an instruction and having it carried out are not the same thing. Inevitably, Alan overlooked this, so, as the staff arrive at the new offices …

Alan: What's going on?
McDonald: The chief fireman won't let us in.
Alan: Well, why won't he?
Fireman: Because the double fire doors have not been fitted on the landings.
Alan: I knew that. I gave *orders* to have it done!

Brutus, who knows a thing or two about following up an instruction, gives them the benefit of his experience:

Brutus: The order not only having been communicated, Alan, imperative it is that it is checked by with or from those people having to perform it.
Alan: Eh?
Brutus: All right. Once you give an order, you must check that it has been carried out. Suppose I had not checked *my* arrangements. Let's see how you would get on at the Forum …

Alan at the Forum.

Alan: Here comes great Caesar now. When I strike, strike with me. Hail Caesar!
Crowd: Hail Caesar!
Caesar: Hail myself! Ahhh …
Alan: Liberty, Freedom. Proclaim it in the market place. Caesar is dead!
Crowd: Caesar is dead!

But he has not *checked*. Caesar sits up:

Caesar: Hello, hello, I want to dial 999, I mean IX, IX, IX …

Brutus points accusingly at Alan:

Brutus: See? Check that your decisions
are carried out correctly, and with
commitment, so that you can put right
anything that's going wrong.

Monty: Right. Let's have a quick re-cap,
shall we? First, collect the facts. Clarify
which decisions are yours, and then
decide what information you need.
Then, go out and get it. Then what?

Alan: Then, consult those affected and
always identify who will be affected by
your decision. Check the facts with
them. Ask them for their opinion, and
listen to it. Then take the decision.
That means gathering all your options
and deciding when you have to decide.
And when that moment comes, be
decisive. If you've got to toss a coin, so
be it, but once you've taken a decision,
be committed to it. Then, communicate
your decision. Be prepared to sell it.
Always brief in a group. And always
confirm in writing. Then people will go
along with your decision, providing that
you've consulted them in the first place.

*... you sent a memo to Mr Owen asking him
to change our sockets on the twenty-fourth of May ...*

Check that your decision
has been carried out.

And finally, check that your decision
has been carried out.

Monty: I think he's got it.

Queen Elizabeth: He hath it.

Monty: Jolly well done.

Churchill: Carry on!

Problems can arise with the correct decisions as well as the incorrect.

Never allow 'routine' to become a synonym for 'thoughtless'.

Don't take a decision you cannot implement.

The decision to take a decision is itself a decision.

Before taking a decision, make sure it's yours to take.

Never be afraid to draw on the experience of others.

In aspects relevant to your decision, you cannot be too well informed.

Never spring a surprise you don't have to.

Consultation is not another word for consensus.

However marginal, be totally committed to a decision once taken.

It sometimes takes courage not to take a decision.

Decisions have to be 'sold' to those affected.

Golden rules

3 Meetings, bloody meetings

Are you like Tim? If so, you spend a lot of time in meetings, usually late for the next because the last one overran. You'll have to work late into the night because the day was full of meetings: you may only have the energy to keep going because of the odd snatch of sleep you manage at those meetings ... Perhaps, like Tim, you actually chair

Before the meeting

The most important question you should ask is: 'What is this meeting intended to achieve?' You can ask it in different ways – 'What would be the likely consequences of not holding it?' 'When it is over, how shall I judge whether it was a success or a failure?' – but unless you have a very clear requirement from the meeting, there is a grave danger that it will be a waste of everyone's time.

Start on time

There is only one way to ensure that a meeting starts on time, and that is to start it on time. Latecomers who find that the meeting has begun without them soon learn the lesson. The alternative is that the prompt and punctual members will soon realize that a meeting never starts until ten minutes after the advertised time, and they will also learn the lesson.

some of those meetings, but perhaps you haven't often asked yourself whether they are all necessary in the first place or whether you are running them effectively. Certainly Tim hasn't. Let's judge him in action through several examples and give a verdict after each. All of us will recognize that the verdicts could apply equally to many of our own performances! First, here he is, late as usual, for a weekly production meeting. His colleagues are waiting impatiently ...

Tim: Sorry I'm late ... just been to the bloody planning meeting ... went on and on as usual. Bloody waste of time. Well, nice to see you all again ... er ... now ...

Ian: How long is it going to take this morning, Tim?

Tim: Depends what we've got to discuss, really.

Ian: Do you mind taking the things you need me for first? I should be on the floor …

Tim: I should think so. Well … nice to see you all again. Gosh, is it really a week since we met? Seems like yesterday.

Jack: It was yesterday.

Tim: What?

Jack: We had to make a decision on the overtime rates.

Tim: So we did! Oh well … Yes. Well, nice to see you all as I say.

David: What are we talking about this morning?

Tim: Yes, we'd better talk about that first. Ian's got to go pretty sharpish, so …

Punctuality at future meetings can be wonderfully reinforced by the practice of listing late arrivals (and early departures) in the minutes. Its ostensible and perfectly proper purpose is to call the latecomer's attention to the fact that he was absent when a decision was reached. Its side-effect, however, is to tell everyone on the circulation list that he was late, and people do not want that sort of information about themselves published too frequently.

Functions of a meeting

1 In the simplest and most basic way, a meeting defines the team, the group or the unit.
2 A meeting is the place where the group revises, updates and adds to what it knows *as a group*.
3 A meeting helps every individual to understand both the collective aim of the group and the way in which his own and everyone else's work can contribute to the group's success.
4 A meeting creates in all present a commitment to the decisions it makes and the objectives it pursues.
5 In the world of management, a meeting is very often the only occasion where the team or group actually exists and works as a group, and the only time when the supervisor, manager or executive is actually perceived as the leader of the team, rather than as the official to whom individuals report.
6 A meeting is a status arena. It is no good to pretend that people are not or should not be concerned with their status relative to the other members in a group.

Ian: Tim, what have you got?
Tim: ... Er ...
David: I'd like to talk about the night-shift standbys.
Jack: That's OK, David, I had a word with Frank.
Tim: Well, what else have we got? I always think it's very useful to get together like this, you know, to see ...
Ian: If there's any point in having got together.
Tim: What?
Ron: Oh Tim, I saw Hawkins on Friday.
Tim: What did he say?
Ron: He thinks we'll be fine until the last quarter. But he did point out that the new cooling system's got problems.
Tim: Well, I've been taking care of that. So, what else have we got to talk about?
Ian: Nothing for me.
Jack: No.
Ron: No.
David: No.
Howard: No.
Tim: Good. Right ...

Verdict

A clear case of chairing a meeting without due thought and preparation. Nobody had anything they wanted to talk about; there was no agenda; the only topics raised were irrelevant to a *meeting*. They could have been dealt with on the telephone or in each other's offices. Yes, it was a regular weekly meeting but a little planning could have enabled Tim to realize that there was no point in having it *as such*. Never have a meeting just because, like Everest, 'it's there'. *Always cancel a meeting, even a regular one, if you can discover it will be a waste of everyone's time.* Ask yourself what would be the consequences of not having it. Remember that conducting a meeting means:

Why have a meeting?

A great many important matters are quite satisfactorily conducted by a single individual who consults nobody. A great many more are resolved by a letter, a memo, a phone call or a simple conversation between two people. Sometimes five minutes spent with six people separately is more effective and productive than a half-hour meeting with them all together. But a meeting still performs functions that will never be taken over by telephones, teleprinters, xerox copiers, tape-recorders, television monitors, or any other technological instruments of the information revolution.

The Company may have closed down, gentlemen, but the first Wednesday of the month still comes round ...

1 preparing yourself so that you are quite clear what the meeting is for
2 making sure that anybody else is clear as well.

Never have a meeting just because it's there.

Define the objective

1 *Informative-digestive.* Obviously, it is a waste of time for a meeting to give out purely factual information that would be better circulated in a document. But if the information should be heard from a particular person, or if it needs some clarification and comment to make sense of it, or if it has deep implications for the members of the meeting, then it is perfectly proper to introduce an item onto the agenda that requires no conclusion, decision or action from the meeting; it is enough, simply, that the meeting should receive and discuss a report.

2 *Constructive-originative.* This 'What shall we do?'

function embraces all items that require something new to be devised, such as a new policy, a new strategy, a new sales target, a new product, a new marketing plan, a new procedure and so forth. This sort of discussion asks people to contribute their knowledge, experience, judgement and ideas.

3 *Executive responsibilities.* This is the 'How shall we do it?' function, which comes after it has been decided what the members are going to do. Here their contribution is the responsibility for implementing the plan.

4 *Legislative framework.* Above and around all considerations of 'What to do' and 'How to do it' there is a framework – a departmental or divisional organization – and a system of rules, routines and procedures within and through which all the activity takes place. Changing this framework and introducing a new organization or new procedures can be deeply disturbing to committee members and a threat to their status and long-term security. Yet leaving it unchanged can stop the organization from adapting to a changing world. At whatever level this change happens, it must have the support of all the perceived leaders whose groups are affected by it.

The second example finds Tim slightly better prepared. At least he has an agenda ...

Tim: Right. Everyone got the agenda? Item One. Improving company communications. I think we all understand the problem. Ron?

Ron: It's a problem all right. It'll cost a lot of money to solve it.

Jack: You mean staff costs?

Ron: No, not staff. Equipment.

Tim: Surely it's management time at the root of it?

Ron: No. Equipment. At least six more video display units –

Tim: What?

Ron: Well if you want Sales and Accounts to have direct access to data, the ...

Tim: Look, Ron, we may be able to deal with this later on if there's time, but can we take Item One now?

Ron: I am taking Item One. Improving company communications.

Jack: No, no Ron, it's not the computer, it's the telephones. Look, every time we try to get through down there, they're engaged.

Tim: No it isn't.

Ron: What?

Tim: I'm talking about the staff briefing sessions. How we brief the staff on this year's company results.

Jack: The company results? I thought you wanted an automated switchboard. You know the hold-ups we've been having down there.

Tim: Look. I'm talking about company communications.

Ron: So am I.

Jack: So am I. How can we communicate if the phone's always busy?

Tim: Look, the whole point of this was to get ideas on how to brief staff on this year's company results.

Ian: Well, why didn't you say so?

Tim: I mean hasn't anyone done any thinking about this ... ?

Verdict

Guilty of failure to signal intentions to the meeting. An agenda is not just a list of headings to remind the Chairman of the topics. It's not a crib card. It's a brief for all the others to work from. It has to define the direction and the area of the discussion and also its end purpose. Tim had an agenda all right, but if an item means something different to each person at the meeting it is worse than useless. The Chairman not only loses control of the meeting, but essential preparatory work will not have been done. All members must be *briefed* so that the agenda becomes common and instantly recognizable ground.

So, make it clear to everybody what is being discussed, why it is being discussed,

Make preparations

People

The value and success of a committee meeting are seriously threatened if too many people are present. Between four and seven is generally ideal, ten is tolerable and twelve is the outside limit. So the Chairman should do everything he can to keep numbers down, consistent with the need to invite everyone with an important contribution to make.

The leader may have to leave out people who expect to come or who have always come. For this job he may need tact; but since people generally preserve a fiction that they are overworked already and dislike serving on committees, it is not usually hard to secure their consent to stay away.

The Agenda

The agenda is by far the most important piece of paper. Properly drawn up, it has a power of speeding and clarifying a meeting that very few people understand or

57

harness. The main fault is to make it unnecessarily brief and vague. The leader should not be afraid of a long agenda, provided that the length is the result of his analyzing and defining each item more closely, rather than of his adding more items than the meeting can reasonably consider in the time allowed. He should also bear in mind the useful device of heading each item 'For information', 'For decision' so that those at the meeting know where they are trying to get to.

The Chairman should not circulate the agenda too far in advance, since the less organized members will forget it or lose it. Two or three days is about right – unless the supporting papers are voluminous.

and what you hope to achieve from the discussion. Anticipate the information you and the others will need and make sure you all have them.

The third meeting sees Tim with a better-planned agenda:

Tim: Right, that's Item One. For decision, allocation of parking spaces in the New Park. Six spaces for Marketing and PR. Four each for Production Management and Works Management. And eight for Admin.

Marcus: For review after three months.

Tim: Yes, yes … God! Did that really take fifty minutes? Right. Item Two. For decision, McKenna order for 250 L3s for delivery by 31 October. Do we accept the order or is 31 October too tight?

Marcus: The L3s are practically obsolete.

Tim: Marcus, they're not obsolete.

The leader may have to leave out people who expect to come to the meeting.

Marcus: Well we oughtn't to be selling them. The L5s are more durable, they're easier to …

Tim: I'm sorry. I want to take this order.

Marcus: I think we're making a mistake.

Tim: Look, I'm sorry. It's ten to …

Marcus: Well if we hadn't spent fifty

minutes discussing the bloody parking …

Tim: That was urgent. The New Park opens on Monday. Ron, how can we do this McKenna job?

Ron: We'll have to do L3s on number 2 and 3 machine, tomorrow and Thursday.

Tim: Right, OK. That's it, then. Now Item Three. For information. Forward Maintenance Schedules for batch-work machines. Ian?

Ian: Nice to get a word in.

Tim: You want to chair this?

Ian: Not *now*. I just want to say I've got to rewire number 2 and 3 machines over the next three nights.

Tim: Oh Christ!

Ian: I warned you last week.

Tim: Won't it wait till the weekend?

Ian: If you don't mind the place going up in smoke.

Tim: What about McKenna's L3s then?

Ian: Your problem.

Tim: Well, why didn't you mention this when we were discussing it?

Ian: I've been trying to.

Tim: … What can we do, Ron?

Marcus: Not take the order.

Ron: We'll have to put number 4 on to the L3s. That'll mean more overtime.

Tim: Right. That's the plan. Any problems about overtime, Bert?

Bert: I'm not sure my members will agree to overtime. You see we're a bit worried about the bonus scheme.

Tim: Right, well … we'll talk about the bonus scheme first now then. Then, if we can get that sorted out, we'll deal with the overtime. Then we can go back to Item Two … and see …

Marcus: Whether to take the McKenna order or not.

Encourage the clash of ideas

A good meeting is not a series of dialogues between individual members and the Chairman. Instead, it is a crossflow of discussion and debate, with the Chairman occasionally guiding, mediating, probing, stimulating and summarizing, but mostly letting the others thrash out ideas. However, the meeting must be a contention of *ideas*, not people.

Remember that once someone of high authority has pronounced on a topic, the less senior members are likely to be inhibited. If you work up the pecking order instead of down it, you are apt to get a wider spread of view and ideas. But the juniors who start it off should only be asked for contributions within their personal experience and competence.

Perhaps you'd like to kick off, Peter, while the others gird their loins ...

Work up the pecking order.

The Chairman's job

If the Chairman is to make sure that the meeting achieves valuable objectives, he will be more effective seeing himself as the servant of the group, rather than as its master. His role then becomes that of assisting the group toward the best conclusion or decision in the most efficient manner possible: to interpret and clarify; to move the discussion forward; and to bring it to a resolution that everyone understands and accepts as being the will of the meeting, even if the individuals do not necessarily agree with it.

Verdict

Negligent ordering of agenda and criminal misallocation of time. Of course parking spaces were urgent and should have been Item One, but not being *important*, they should have been polished off in five minutes. The Chairman could even have put 'five minutes' against it on the agenda. Far worse was Tim's attempt to decide whether to accept an order before establishing that the men and machines were available to do it. Always look for logical connections between different items *and arrange them in the necessary order*. And allocate time so that the important items, even if they are the least urgent, get the fullest discussion.

The next example shows Tim handling a difficult problem:

Tim: Right, Item Four. Discipline. I don't think there are too many problems but I've got to review the discipline agreements with Bert this week, so what does anyone think?

Marcus: Well, they're still nicking knives and forks from the canteen.

David: I thought that had stopped.

Marcus: Oh it stopped, yes, for about ten

minutes.

David: Well you expect a bit of that. How much is it going on?

Marcus: Enough.

Ron: My problem is that people are still clocking on for each other.

Ian: What your lads need, Ron, is a bit of discipline.

David: It depends what you mean by discipline.

Marcus: I'll tell you what I mean by discipline. Nailing a few of them to the front gates – that's what I mean by ...

David: Oh shut up, Marcus. What I'm getting at is there won't be much of your kind of discipline till we get the hygiene factors right.

Ron: Well, which ones are still wrong?

David: Look, are we talking about problems or solutions? Because if it's solutions, we should start with trying to shorten discipline procedures.

Tim: Well, I think we've got to review the problems first.

Ron: OK. Well, here's one. Now can we really expect a supervisor to control a group of forty-five?

Marcus: I'll tell you the problem. We can't even control the bloody supervisors.

Ron: They're all right.

Ian: So are mine. Good lads. I scratch their backs and they scratch mine.

Ron: No, it's much more a question of giving them fewer men to supervise.

Marcus: I'll tell you what's the problem. They're bone bloody idle. We ought to sack a few. That'd wake them up.

David: And get another Jones case.

Ron: Amazing, wasn't it? He was absolutely useless.

David: But we couldn't prove it, could we?

Verdict

A total neglect of structure and control. Tim hasn't presided over a discussion at all, it was more like a group therapy session. Discussions have to be structured, from the chair. First, state the proposition; second, produce

Structure the discussion

It may seem that there is no right way or wrong way to structure a committee-meeting discussion. A subject is raised, people say what they think, and finally a decision is reached, or the discussion is terminated. There is some truth in this. Moreover, it would be a mistake to try to tie every discussion of every item down to a single immutable format.

Nevertheless, there is a logical order to a group discussion, and while there can be reasons for not following it, there is no justification for not being aware of it.

A simple example – if the item is at all complex or especially significant, it is important for the Chairman not only to have the proposed course of the discussion in his own head, but also to announce it so that everyone knows.

Perhaps one of the most common faults of chairmanship is the failure to terminate the discussion early enough. Sometimes Chairmen do not realize that the meeting has effectively reached an agreement, and consequently they let the discussion go on for another few minutes, getting nowhere at all. Even more often, they are not quick enough to close a discussion *before* agreement has been reached.

At the end of the discussion of each agenda item, the Chairman should give a brief and clear summary of what has been agreed on. This can act as the dictation of the actual minutes. It serves not merely to put the item on record, but also to help people realize that something worthwhile has been achieved. It also answers the question: 'Where did all that get us?' If the summary involves action by a member of the meeting, he should be asked to confirm his acceptance of the undertaking.

the evidence and by all means allow arguments about what the evidence proves; third, come to a conclusion, and only then is the meeting in a position to decide on the action which should be taken in the light of that conclusion. Evidence must come before the interpretation of evidence, and interpretation before a decision on action. It is vital to keep these stages separate and to prevent people riding pet hobby-horses or going over old ground without regard to the proper sequence.

Finally, let's see how Tim handles a meeting which depends on the accurate recording of information and decisions deriving from a previous meeting.

Tim: OK. Last item. Ian, can you bring us up to date on progress on the pay structure review?

Ian: Well I haven't been able to take it any further really. I can't till the joint negotiating committee meets and decides about the regrading claims. When are they going to meet, David?

David: But George was going to arrange that, wasn't he? He wanted to be there to put his case.

Tim: Ian, I thought you were going to fix a meeting quickly as you needed to know.

Ian: But Ron usually does that.

David: Usually, yes, but as George said he wanted to be in on it we said we'd leave it to him.

Ron: That's what I thought. We left it to George.

Ian: But George isn't here. I thought it was you, Ron.

Ron: No. George.

Ian: Would you like to take a vote on it?

Howard: Surely we decided that Ian would coordinate with George and Ron?

Kinds of meetings

1 The *daily meeting*, where people work together on the same project with a common objective and reach decisions informally by general agreement.
2 The *weekly* or *monthly meeting*, where members work on different but parallel projects and where there is a certain competitive element and a greater likelihood that the chairman will make the final decision himself.
3 The *irregular*, *occasional* or *'special project'* meeting, composed of people whose normal work does not bring them into contact and whose work has little or no relationship to the others. They are united only by the project the meeting exists to promote and motivated by the desire that the project should succeed.

Record the meeting

Although the Chairman is unlikely to take them personally – indeed it is usually better if he doesn't – he is nonetheless accountable for the minutes. They can be very brief, but they should include these facts:

1 The time and date of the meeting, where it was held and who chaired it.
2 Names of all present and apologies for absence.
3 All agenda items (and other items) discussed and all decisions reached. If action was agreed on, record (and underline) the name of the person responsible for the assignment.
4 The main arguments leading to decisions.
5 The time at which the meeting ended (important, because it may be significant later to know whether the discussion lasted fifteen minutes or six hours).
6 The date, time and place of the next committee meeting.

Tim: We agreed to take the necessary action.
Jack: Which meant Ron would make sure the committee consulted George.
Ron: Not in this case. It was George's job.
Tim: Next item. Item Eleven. To discuss and decide exactly what we did discuss and decide at the last meeting.
Ron: Before we decide that …
Tim: Well?
Ron: … oughtn't George to be here?
Tim: But I thought everybody knew what had been decided …

Verdict

A clear case of failure to summarize and record. Always summarize all decisions at a meeting, clearly and concisely, and make certain everyone has a chance to raise a point they are in doubt about. Then record the decisions immediately with the name of the person or group of persons responsible for any action. Ironically, a forum which, at its best, is a vehicle for communication can too easily become one which leads to the opposite.

Ask yourself what would be the consequences of *not* meeting.

If you discover that a meeting will be a
waste of time – cancel it.

An agenda is not a crib-card for the
Chairman.

A meeting should be about a contention of
ideas, not people.

Arrange the agenda in a logical order.

The Chairman is a servant of a group, not
a master.

Confirm the action points to be followed
by members of the meeting, and record
them.

Golden rules

4 Who's in charge? The supervisor's role

Companies, especially large ones, can be a labyrinth of departments, sections and divisions with a multiplicity of staff employed with varying degrees of managerial responsibility from the top executive to the foreman and supervisors who look after the groups who comprise 'the shop floor'. The supervisor level is one whose importance is easily overlooked by the more senior levels of management, and the responsibilities of which can be similarly neglected by the supervisors themselves.

Supervisors, whether of the workers on an assembly belt or of a typing pool, are in charge of a *team*. As such they have responsibilities downwards and upwards – to represent the interests of their team and its members to the more senior level, and to represent the requirements and decisions of senior management to their own staff.

No good manager should divorce himself or herself from the work of their supervisors, partly because within the company it is a vital 'interface' role between management and worker and therefore vital to the smooth running of the organization, and partly because if the supervisor's work is not adequately discharged, essential business can be easily disrupted.

Are these principles easy to follow? Take a girl like Liz, who works in the sales accounts office of Glendower, Douglas and Scroop. She is an intelligent and likeable woman in her mid-twenties who has been working for the company as a costing clerk. She has experience of computers and has been chosen by her boss, Humphrey Mortimer, to run the office team in the sales accounts section. Suddenly she finds herself in charge of half a dozen clerks who, the day before, were her equals. She needs to get them to accept her and the changes she has to make, and also to satisfy Humphrey Mortimer and his boss, Harry Lancaster, that she can deliver the work. Liz has to do a number of things at once. She has to explain why the new computing system has been chosen and show the others what they will have to do. At the same time she has to advise and encourage each member of staff personally and make sure that they are all pulling their weight. And she has to do a fair share of the work herself, as well as leading the rest of the team. Not an easy situation – especially for someone without any experience of managing other people. Let's see how Humphrey Mortimer prepared her for her new position:

Mortimer: Ah, Miss Travers, come in. Shut the door if you would. Sit down. So, are you enjoying computers?

Liz: Very much.

Mortimer: Good. I wanted to have a quiet word with you. You know Mrs Blunt's leaving?

Liz: I knew she was away.

Mortimer: Yes. Her husband's had a stroke, poor man, and she's going to have to spend her time nursing him. The point is, she won't be coming back. And we'd like you to take over.

Liz: What do you mean, take over?

Mortimer: Well, I'd like you to take the post. You know the work. You know the new methods. You're acquainted with everyone in the office, aren't you?

Liz: But I don't have any experience of supervisory work.

Mortimer: Oh, you'll manage. You'll pick it up as you go along. I'm behind you. You don't want to spend the rest of your life number-crunching, do you? I know you think, like I do, that the only way to achieve this reorganization is to move as swiftly as we can to on-line computing. I think you could handle that, couldn't you?

Liz: Yes, I think I could. I'll give it a try.

Mortimer: Well, there's no time like the
present, is there?
Liz: Right.

That was terrible! Liz has received no
proper training or backing from the management above her, so she is bound to make
mistakes. It is up to management, in the first
place, to make sure that supervisors like Liz
are fully trained and prepared for the job,
and given adequate support and advice while
they are doing it. Had Mortimer followed
certain elementary guidelines, their conversation would have been totally different.
There are five important points for managers
to bear in mind when they are appointing
supervisors:

1 Choose and prepare your supervisors
  carefully and introduce them adequately
  to their staff.
2 Make clear to them the scope and limits
  of their responsibilities and precisely to
  whom they are responsible.
3 Ensure that they understand and
  communicate their team's objectives.
4 Insist on their loyalty both to
  management and to their team.
5 Give them continual guidance and
  support; set aside, as a matter of
  routine, time for properly prepared
  consultation with your supervisors.

But, as we have seen, Humphrey
Mortimer followed none of these principles.
He did not even bother to tell Liz's team of
her appointment, or explain to her what her
specific function and responsibilities would
be. Inevitably, difficulties soon arise in the
office. Pam, who has been keeping the sales
ledger for Mr Mortimer, resents having
responsibility taken away from her, and is
jealous of Liz's promotion. On the other
hand, Kathy, in charge of invoicing, will find
she has too much to do. The junior clerks,

like Val and Percy, are worried about being made redundant by the new computing system:

Val: Will Mrs Blunt be coming back, do you think?

Liz: No, her husband's in a pretty bad way, I'm afraid.

Percy: Here. Do you reckon the firm will take care of her? Or do you think they'll just pass the hat around?

Liz: I don't know.

Pam: What do you mean Percy?

Percy: Stands to reason, doesn't it, with all this automation. Less staff, it's easy.

Pam: Do you think anybody will lose their job, Liz?

Liz: I don't know.

Kathy: Oh come on. Mortimer must have told you something.

Liz: You know what he's like. Mortimer didn't say anything to me at all.

Val: He wouldn't. Typical.

Liz: Yes, typical. They're all men, aren't they?

Liz is making fatal mistakes here. By not being loyal to the managers above her, she is helping to undermine everyone's confidence in the organization. At a time when radical new methods are being introduced, this is particularly serious. And now she is going to undermine her staff too by appearing, as she introduces them to the new computer methods, to be altering their responsibilities in an arbitrary way.

Liz: … So, Val, you enter the account number and that gives you what is in the ledger at the moment, see? And if you want to change an entry you simply key it in.

Val: Good as the telly, isn't it?

Pam: You've done it wrong now. That's not the proper figure.

Liz: It doesn't matter. I can erase it.

Val: Oh, I'm never going to get the hang of this, you know.

Liz: Of course you will, Val. It's very easy. You okay Pam?

Pam: Yes, I think so. It's like a calculator, really.

Liz: You might think so but it's more than a calculator. As well as storing what you input, it'll print it out in any order you like.

Pam: And I just take the printouts to Mr Mortimer?

Liz: No, you bring them to me.

Pam: What? I always take the ledger figures straight to Mr Mortimer. And the analyses.

Liz: But I'll have to agree the totals before Mr Mortimer sees them.

Pam: But Mrs Blunt never used to. She always used to leave that to me.

Liz: Well, she wasn't used to working this way. In future I'll set up the schedules and leave you to get the information from the computer. It'll be very easy.

Pam: Yes, I'm sure. What am I supposed to do with the rest of my time? Twiddle my thumbs?

Liz: No, I'd like you to help Val. Give her a hand till she's got the hang of all this.

Pam: And by that time she'll be off having her baby. I'll just be left updating all the records.

Liz: Only temporarily …

Terrible again. Pam's confidence has been shaken, long-standing friendships have begun to suffer, rumours and petty jealousies have started to replace effective leadership and communication. Getting nowhere with Liz, Pam feels she has no alternative but to take her problems to Mortimer, further weakening normal chains of command. How will Mortimer respond?

Pam: … I don't mind helping out, you ought to know that. It's a question of responsibility. I used to bring my work to you. Now I have to take it to Liz Travers.

Mortimer: Yes, well, these are the new routines.

Pam: But she gives her mate Kathy responsible work to do. She doesn't give it to me.

Mortimer: Well, you'll have to sort that out between you.

Pam: What about Val? Are you going to replace her or have I got to do her share of the work?

Mortimer: Well, that is entirely Liz's responsibility.

Pam: So there *are* going to be redundancies!

Mortimer: Ah, well, we certainly oughtn't to need more staff. I'm very busy. Look, give it a chance, Pam, and will you please just try to let things settle down for a few days and help out where you can. I've got a lot on my plate at the minute.

Yes, once again Mortimer is letting Liz down. And also Pam. He should be attempting to reconcile Pam to the new arrangements rather than making things worse by refusing to listen to her properly. And he certainly should have scotched any talk of redundancies. Meanwhile, back in the sales accounts office, Liz is adding to the problems:

Val: Liz, about my maternity leave. The firm are supposed to take me back after the baby's born, aren't they?

Liz: I believe so.

Problems and grievances

Nothing undermines group morale more quickly than an individual with a problem, or a problem with an individual. In either case, performance is frequently impaired – and when one team member stops pulling his weight, everyone's performance is inevitably affected. A well-knit group becomes sensitive to these issues, and when the supervisor does not spot them and act quickly, it notices and can react very swiftly. It may not stop work – but it can easily stop working as a team, which is a much more subtle way of demonstrating resentment. Individual members and their problems together make up one of your prime responsibilities.

The colour coding system makes her dizzy ...

Individual members and their problems are one of your prime responsibilities.

Val: Well, can I count on that? I'm not very good on that computer and, well, the thing is I want to come back as soon as possible. Stan's not getting much work now and we're going to have all this expense with the baby and ...

Liz: Look, Val, it's really not my department. Why don't you go down and talk to Admin.?

Val: Will you be keeping my present job open?

Liz: I don't know, Val. Go and talk to Admin. I've got all this work to do for Mr Mortimer.

Liz should not have brushed aside Val's genuine concerns as if they were simply too trivial for her to get involved with. Even if she didn't know the answer to the question, she should have appreciated its importance, shared it, and made it her own business to discover both the legal position and the company's attitude to Val's wish to return after maternity leave.

As leader of the team, you must expect people to come to you for advice. Indeed, you should be worried if they don't. It may not always be convenient or easy; but it is an obligation of your position as well as an act of friendship. You can help simply by being a good listener. People with a genuine problem often have no one with whom they can discuss it, though you will have to learn to differentiate between those with a real need and those who like a moan – which is a need in itself.

Members of your team will come to value your advice if you can offer useful suggestions (such as putting them in touch with welfare services), but not if you make unrealistic promises which are not followed up; and they will respect it more if they know that you always tell them the facts, even when they are unpalatable. Above all, they will appreciate your confidentiality: they may talk about it to the others, but will not expect you to.

It's worth remembering, though, that unsought advice is usually less welcome, and bad advice is obviously worse than none. So, think carefully before you speak about what is probably very important to the other person.

In this Liz has failed Val. In fact, she is failing all the way along the line. Already, as we have seen, Pam is jealous of the 'responsible' work given to Kathy; but has Liz checked to see how Kathy is coping with her invoices and other tasks under the new system? Following Pam's complaints, Mortimer feels impelled to have a word with Liz:

Mortimer: Pam Vernon's been in here complaining about the work you've been giving her.
Liz: I only asked her to help Val …
Mortimer: Pam's an excellent worker but she's a bit touchy. You do realize she was after the supervisor's job herself?
Liz: No, I didn't realize.
Mortimer: Yes. So please watch how you go with her. I've got enough to do at the moment without people coming in

Shoulder responsibility

One of the most difficult parts of the supervisor's job, perhaps the most difficult of all, is accepting that you are responsible to your own boss for achieving results, and for getting individual team members to act in the best interests of the business. It is not possible to be the team leader and to cop out from shouldering responsibility for the team's work. The fact is that almost every group of people – whether at work or not – needs to be led.

The first principle of leading a team lies in fully accepting the responsibility for it. This means not only taking the bad with the good, it also means being prepared to involve yourself in human problems which were once not your concern; in the role of supervisor they will be your unavoidable responsibility.

Don't pass the buck

The supervisor's job usually involves managing an operative team in an organization, and for that very reason is probably one of the most crucial jobs in management. But it is, nevertheless, management. No supervisor can function effectively and side with the group he leads against management. Accepting responsibility for carrying out an objective set by higher management implies being loyal to the people and the motives of those responsible for that decision. To take the attitude, 'Don't blame me. It was their idea,' is to abdicate the role of leader.

But there are two sides to the coin. When the supervisor in his role of leader needs to represent his group and their problems to management, he has no option but to be loyal to his group in giving their views. He has no more right to blame the team beneath him for their incompetencies than he has to blame the management for theirs. Loyalty must operate upwards and downwards. It's a tricky balance to maintain, and it's what makes the job important.

and out of here with silly office squabbles. It is your job to see that everything out there runs smoothly.

Liz: What happened, Mr Mortimer, is …

Mortimer: I don't want to know. I'll leave all that to you.

Liz: Did you tell Pam to do what I asked her?

Mortimer: Well … no … I merely suggested that she should help out where she could. And incidentally, you do realize that there are errors in these customer invoices …

So Mortimer has abdicated yet again. He has not demonstrated his support and backing for Liz; he has taken no initiative to discuss the workload problem with her; he has given her no advice. All he has done is to say, 'Things are bad, it's your job to deal with them', and pointed out the mistakes on the invoices without, of course, any discussion about how the errors are arising and what could be done to make improvements. It is an angry and worried Liz who rushes back to her department.

Liz: I hear you've been making complaints about me to Mr Mortimer.

Pam: I told him what was going on.

Liz: You'd no right …

Pam: I can talk to Mr Mortimer if I want. I always have done.

Liz: Not behind my back. If you have any complaints, you can make them to me. And Kathy! I'd like a word with you. There are several mistakes in these invoice entries. You do check them, don't you?

Kathy: Yes I do. As much as I've time for.

Liz: Then I'd better check them too, in future.

Liz is now desperately trying to assert her

authority, instead of listening to, and thinking about, Pam's and Kathy's complaints. She has not delegated properly, so the workload in the office is unfairly spread. It is not surprising that Kathy is making mistakes. The answer is not to attack Kathy for the errors, but to find a way of redistributing the work that is acceptable to everyone. Liz should also attempt to give credit where it is due. Everybody in the office is battling with an unfamiliar system, and it is a trying time for them all. As it is, things in the office are going from bad to worse:

Liz: Mr Mortimer says you're terribly behind with this month's customer accounts.

Kathy: Are we?

Liz: You know you are, Kathy. I don't know what you've all been doing.

Kathy: Well I can't cope any more. I'm doing half Mrs Blunt's work already.

Liz: It depends how you allocate your other work, Kathy.

Kathy: It isn't up to me to allocate it. I'm not the supervisor. No one seems to work around here except me.

Liz: We'll have to try a new system.

Kathy: Well, you can try it without me.

Liz: All right, if that's how you feel. Pam, I want you to give me a hand checking these customer statements.

Pam: I can't now.

Liz: Why not?

Pam: Because I'm off. I've done all my work. Anyway, Mr Mortimer said whenever I finished early I could push off. It's no good trying to ask him. He's gone off to a meeting.

Liz: Look, Pam, the office doesn't close for nearly an hour. If we get down to this together we can finish it.

Pam: I've got a date, I'm sorry.

Avoid the grapevine

The grapevine in a company is inevitable, but its effects can be very damaging. Rumours tend to be concentrated on aspects of a highly emotional nature – whose head is on the chopping block, impending redundancies and so on – and they get distorted in the telling. A good manager must be aware of the dangers and, whether using the notice board, memoranda or oral communication, will make the position crystal clear and so minimize all opportunities for the grapevine to flourish.

By now it is clear to everyone that the situation is desperate, and Liz gets summoned to Mortimer's office.

Mortimer: This office seems to have become a complete shambles since you took over. I've got a letter here from Kathy. It's a notice of resignation. She's one of our best clerks. And we've been informed that the union have made a complaint that members of our section have been threatened with redundancy. Is that true?

Liz: No, but there were rumours.

Mortimer: It is your job to scotch rumours. The company's given a clear undertaking that there'll be no redundancies as a result of this automation. And why isn't the revenue survey ready? It's wanted in for the accountants today.

Liz: I didn't have time.

Mortimer: You should have asked someone like Pam to help you or something.

Liz: She refused.

Mortimer: Refused?

Liz: Yes. She walked out.

Mortimer: Look … if she refused, without reason, you should have reported it. You know, there was never any trouble like this when Mrs Blunt was in charge.

Liz: Well, if you feel I'm not up to it, I'd better go back to my old job as a costing clerk.

Liz Travers was unable to lead her team properly, mainly because no one had told her how to do it. As a result, instead of being its centre she found herself an outsider.

A few guidelines will help the supervisor, at any level, to avoid that fate. To start with, make sure that you are delegating the work

Good grief! The collapse of the Protestant Work Ethic and I missed it!

Keep in touch.

sensibly and fairly, by being careful not to overload willing horses or to withhold responsibility from others. And try to arrange the work so that everyone is contributing to the best of their ability.

A lot of the work will be repetitive and boring – 'number-crunching' in the case of an accounts office like Liz's – but you can make it more attractive and less tedious by conveying your own interest in it to the others. 'Giving a lead' is important, and make sure they know *why* your team is having to do it. Although you may not feel it, you are part of the management now, and must be seen to support it. Undermining the company's authority only serves to undermine your own.

The other side of the coin is that your team should know that you will represent them fully and fairly if they have a genuine complaint or reasonable criticism: loyalty has to go both ways. Because Liz was not able to discuss her staff's problems effectively with them or with Mortimer, in the end they blew up in her face.

If, unlike her, you face the difficulties as they crop up, you may find yourself involved in a tough decision or a tough interview, but the chances are that your team will be as relieved as you are once the decision is made, provided you have been seen to act with good sense and tact. As you and your team get to

Keeping in touch

Obviously, you cannot be in the section the whole time, but it is vital to divide up your activities in such a way as to enable you to be there enough to become accepted as part of the normal everyday activity. At least part of every day should be spent walking around, talking to team members about what they do, helping with technical problems and observing people's behaviour.

If you're familiar with the normal atmosphere in the section, you can always tell when something's wrong. When it's working efficiently it has a 'buzz' about it. But if the 'buzz' isn't there, if everyone is going about their jobs just a bit more slowly, you will only spot its absence if you're out there.

know and understand each other better,
you'll find that leadership will become a
natural part of your job.

In the end, problems like Liz's will
rebound not only on her but on her boss. In
this case, Mortimer gets, and deserves, a
lecture from his own boss, Harry Lancaster.
It is clear to Lancaster where the real fault
lies:

Lancaster: This girl you chose to take
Mrs Blunt's place, Elizabeth Travers,
had she any training?

Mortimer: Well, no, not so much training
as a lot of clerical experience.

Lancaster: But had she any computer
training?

Mortimer: Yes, she'd worked on the
computer.

Lancaster: And had she any training as a
supervisor?

Mortimer: … I didn't think. It was a
matter of time; it was an emergency
appointment.

Lancaster: I appreciate that, Humphrey,
but did you explain to the girl what her
duties and responsibilities were going to
be?

Mortimer: Well, I didn't think there was
any need, since she'd worked in the
office before.

Lancaster: Yes, but not as a supervisor.
Did you introduce her to the rest of the
staff?

Mortimer: She had worked very closely
with them before.

Lancaster: But not as a supervisor! I
mean this appointment is damned
important. Don't you realize this girl is
at the interface between management
and workers. I mean, good God, we're
working in a sophisticated industry
and we're in a damned tough
market.

Lancaster tells Mortimer that it won't do any good to accept Liz's resignation – they can't keep chopping and changing supervisors. The full impact of his failures is brought home to Mortimer, and he is a changed man when he next meets Liz:

Mortimer: Mr Lancaster's view is that we should work things out between us. He wants you to stay on in the post.

Liz: But it hasn't worked.

Mortimer: He thinks you've not been given enough support and advice. He wants us to go over the ground together and try to sort it out.

Liz: Right. I'll try.

Mortimer: So we're agreed, then? Don't try to do everything on your own, and come to me if you've got any difficulties. I think we should get the section together and have a chat to them.

Liz: I think I might prefer to do that on my own.

Mortimer: Fine. Then talk to Kathy and Pam alone. Feel free to use my office. But do get the full team together soon, won't you.

Liz: Thank you, I will.

Mortimer: You see, people in our position can't afford to back away from problems. You must listen to what they say, of course, but at the end of the day you are the one with the responsibility. You can come to me if you've got any problems, because I'll back you up.

Liz: Even when I'm wrong?

Mortimer: If I think you're wrong, then I'll talk to you about it afterwards when we're on our own. All right? Have a go.

Later, in the sales accounts office.

Liz: I think I owe you all an apology. It

Team meetings

Everybody in the team needs to know what is happening that is likely to affect their jobs. There has to be a means of finding out the news. 'How are we doing? What changes are taking place? Who's coming? Who's going?' But all too often, these questions are asked of the wrong people, a sure way of getting the wrong answers. In this way, the grapevine flourishes, rumours grow and gossip-mongers find plenty of willing ears. The sure way of countering the grapevine and of providing correct information is to hold a supervisor's team meeting. Not only will such a meeting provide an occasion for question and answer, it will also serve the critically important function of allowing the team members to express their views. Listening to grievances and problems is the first step in preventing or solving them. And listening to suggestions is the first step in making a team member feel valued for his or her contributions.

Make sure the team knows its objectives

It is self-evident that one of the key elements of success is knowing exactly what you are aiming at. Yet many teams have little more than a very superficial set of goals to aim for.

It is vital to ensure that everyone knows the 'goal'. Try writing it down and remember to discuss it first, rather than simply to impose it. And remember to take into account external factors, beyond the simple production or service process, e.g. quality, quantity, time and cost.

Training on the job

Most teams frequently depend on supervisors for technical help and advice. And the best way of providing this kind of support is by making sure that there is a regular opportunity for discussing each team member's job with him or her.

As a result of this, you can

seems I haven't been doing my new job very well.

Percy: Well, it hasn't been easy for any of us.

Liz: What the management have told me is that there'll be no redundancies, no down-grading, so please don't worry about that. Obviously this new system has added its own difficulties. But believe me it really can be a good system if we can just make it work. Obviously there are flaws at the moment. I'm sure you must have some ideas how we can make it better.

Kathy: Well, I was wondering if we should divide up the invoicing differently.

Liz: Divide it up?

Kathy: We could each take a batch of customers and be responsible for them – including the debt-collecting.

Percy: Up to a certain point when we'd refer them to you. It'd make it much more interesting. We could do our own filing as well.

Liz: Pam, what do you think? It would relieve you of Val's work and give you more time for an analysis.

Pam: So we're staying now, are we, Kathy?

Kathy: Oh, I'd stay if we did it like that.

Liz: Pam?

Pam: I never said anything about leaving, did I?

Anyone who leads a team needs to communicate with them. Half poor Liz's problems arose because she didn't get all her office staff together at the beginning and talk the job through with them. If she had, she'd have understood better why Pam and Kathy were worried about their workloads and why Val and Percy were worried about redundancies. Naturally, she couldn't know all the answers, but she could have found out from other members of management who did know.

There's little use, of course, in consulting your staff unless you pass on the findings, very easily establish an on-the-job training programme, which can be used not only for introducing someone to a job but also for transferring someone from one job to another or for developing a particular skill or aptitude.

There are many benefits in taking an interest in training. Not only does it encourage greater efficiency and job satisfaction, it also helps to establish the supervisor's credibility. A team member who sees that his boss is technically competent inevitably develops greater respect for him.

Understanding the job

It is vital for supervisors to ensure that each member of the team knows where he fits in and what contribution he is expected to make to the common objective. Once again, this is not necessarily a simple matter of agreeing or setting a quantity target. It is also a question of explaining the existence of other yardsticks and agreeing with individuals acceptable standards of performance for them.

Everybody needs to know what is expected of him and where he fits into the scheme of things. If he doesn't, it is easy for him either to opt out or fail to make the best use of his abilities.

Wow! Cool!

A team member who sees that his boss is technically competent develops greater respect for him.

and any queries that they raise, to your boss. It's preferable for him to know what's going on and what people are thinking because you tell him, rather than finding himself faced with unexpected crises. And communication should run sideways, as well as upwards and downwards. It's all too easy, within the confines of your office, to ignore what's happening in other departments and have no idea how your work fits in with the rest. By keeping in touch with your colleagues, the other supervisors, and comparing notes with them, you'll be able to plan your own tasks more intelligently and keep your team more fully aware of the importance and relevance of what they're doing.

Remember, success in leading people is never complete. Things will always go wrong, however hard you try. Nevertheless, the difficulties can be overcome by taking initiatives. Even if you think nobody will let you experiment with an innovation that appears to make sense, at least go and ask. If you don't know how to organize a team meeting, go and talk to someone who already does. And if you don't have the time for some of the actions you think are important, try to identify some routine tasks which could be delegated, in order to give you more scope.

And finally, try to bear in mind one last thought. The job may be difficult and occasionally thankless. But to those who do it well, it can be rewarding and pay dividends. Somebody has to be in charge, after all. Why shouldn't it be you?

Communicating upwards

Communicating well with the team you lead – giving it the information it needs and listening to its views – is vital. But so is the need to communicate in the opposite direction and to feed upwards the information which tells those above what your team is doing. As supervisor you are the first member of line management in constant contact with your team. Managers further up the line, therefore, are heavily dependent on you for correct and complete information about the progress and the abilities, the strengths and the weaknesses of the team you lead. Without it, they cannot make their decisions sensibly.

Golden rules

Loyalty must operate upwards and downwards.

Be aware of the grapevine and minimize its effort.

Individuals with a problem should be regarded as a management responsibility.

Respect confidentiality.

Leading a team means accepting responsibility for it and its performance.

Remember to give credit where it's due.

Give a lead through your own technical competence.

A supervisor is the interface between management and staff.

Teams, like individuals, need to know what is expected of them and the context in which they are working.

Are your business letters clear, concise, polite and to the point? Lawyers and bureaucrats are, of course, notorious for making theirs incomprehensible, but that is no reason for the businessman or woman to follow suit. Moreover, letter-writing is *important*; not only because the letters are often an exchange of views and information – a dialogue – but because they are a permanent record about which there can be no misunderstanding. What you actually said or meant on the telephone can be the subject of argument, but no one can argue with what is in your letter. Moreover, you can copy a letter to others for information or action; not so with a phone call.

So, how would your letters stand up to scrutiny? Are you ever careless?

Dear Sir,
If you think our products are unsatisfactory you should see our manager.

Dear Sir,
In reply to your letter, I have already cohabited with your office, so far without result.

Dear Sir,
I am happy to provide Miss Jones with a reference. She has performed well in all positions in the bank, but has proved to perform particularly well over the counter.

Letter-writing is pretty well always a chore, and the business letter can be particularly hard, both for the receiver and the sender. One problem of a business letter is that you probably know the jargon of your trade, but does the person to whom you are writing know?

Dear Sir,
We should have the layouts for the Company Report available next week. The

5 The business letter business

Why write

The point of a letter is that it does what a visit or phone call can't always do. It not only gets your message across clearly but it provides a permanent record of that message. There can be no misunderstanding, as is possible on the phone or in conversation.

What you actually said or meant on the phone can be the subject of argument, but no one can argue with what is in your letter. In most businesses letters are circulated to other departments for their information, something that a visit or phone call clearly cannot do.

illustration we were sent for the cover has been examined by our designers and they have decided to bleed from the bottom ...

Such a letter *might* be sent to the Chief Executive of a large company who *might* not know that the designers intend to extend the illustration all the way down the cover without a margin!

Here is another example:

Dear Sirs,
Your letter of the 20th is to hand. With reference to your request for remuneration in regard to, and in the matter concerning, our recent acquisition of a number of items viz: thirty thousand three-centimetre self-adjusting grummet flanges. It is felt within these purlieus that in the majority of instances there is a negative aspect to their usefulness to this company so therefore I very much regret that no payment can, at this moment in time, be made. Our Chief Engineer is of the opinion that, and I concur that, the aforementioned thirty thousand three-centimetre self-adjusting grummet flanges are substantially inadequate in the fact that they are only 2.583 centimetres in diameter, and are not, one ventures to say, 'self-adjusting', and are not, you may be surprised to learn, in fact, grummet flanges, but, I am reliably informed, grummet filters. I look forward to an expression of your views on this strange state of affairs in subsequent correspondence.
Yours, etc.

Not so much trade jargon here; instead the writer has simply swallowed a dictionary and the recipient can't be expected to use one to understand 'negative aspect of their usefulness', or 'viz', or 'purlieus'. Is it any wonder that with such a convoluted style the com-

Make it clear

If your letters are to produce results, it is essential that the person to whom you are writing should understand what you are saying. That is why the language you use must be clear and simple. There is no excuse for decorating your letters with phrases such as *'plus ça change, plus c'est la même chose'*. It's not only bad letter-writing, it's stuffy, archaic and rather snobbish.

On the other hand, slang and contemporary jargon are equally to be avoided. 'Say no more squire', 'get my drift', 'a touch of the other', 'stone me', are not phrases that would come instantly to mind when writing a business letter. The worst enemy of better letter-writing is still the archaic cliché. 'Esteemed command', 'cherished favours of early replies', and 'assurances of best intentions' belong with high collars and quill pens back in the nineteenth century.

Letter-writing types

When it comes to dictation, business men and women divide up into several types.

First and best are those who are prepared – who come to a session of dictation with their letters in rough draft or note form. But there are many other types too. There are those who dictate 'off the top of the head' and who leave it to the secretary to sort out the resultant confusion.

Then there are the over-verbose, the 'swallowed the dictionary' types who never use a one-syllable word when there are three- or four-syllable words available. Often their letters require translation into plain English.

There are many business people who, having dictated their letters, have second thoughts when the secretary brings them in for signature. They virtually rewrite their letters, which might be bully for them but it means that the secretary has to do everything twice – a waste of time, money and patience.

Then, of course, horror of horrors, there are the dictators who combine all of these faults and whose biggest annual turnover is secretaries.

pany received filters instead of flanges? It will go out of business quickly if nobody understands what it wants.

Bosses probably have little idea of the contempt their letters, dictated or written, inspire in their secretaries. Here is a secretary describing a variety of letter-writers she has known:

'There's what you could call the "off the top of the head" ones. The "no preparation, eyes down, leave the secretary to sort it out later later" type'. She recalls a typical example:

Businessman: Dear whatever his name is, where the hell are our spare parts? God knows it's hard enough making ends meet without idiots like you screwing things up. So let's be having you p.d.q.
> Yours, etc.

Read that back would you?

Secretary: Dear Mr Foster, I'm sorry to inform you that the spare parts we ordered on form 02/593/27 have still not arrived. I'd be grateful to learn

Can it unscramble dictations?

There are those who dictate 'off the top of the head' and leave it to the secretary to sort out the resultant confusion.

when we can expect them.
        Yours sincerely.
Businessman: Yes, that's fine.

Now, an example of those who never use a short word when a long one will do:

Businessman: It is commensurate with

Useful aids

The business letter-writer should always have to hand a dictionary and a copy of Roget's *Thesaurus*. A thesaurus is 'a book containing systemised lists of synonymous and related words', which is another way of saying you can find an alternative word to the word 'alternative' and thus avoid repetition. The following books may prove useful:

Roget's *Thesaurus*
(Longmans)

The Complete Plain Words by Sir Ernest Gowers (H.M.S.O. and Penguin)
Usage and Abusage (Hamish Hamilton)
The Business Man's Guide to Letter Writing and *The Law on Letters* by Greville Janner (Business Books)
A Guide to the Writing of Business Letters (B.A.C.I.E.)
A Guide to Letter Writing (The Industrial Society)
Pocket Guide to Written English by Michael Temple (John Murray)

our policy relating to the contractual proviso of our purchasing agreements. We must conclude, however unaccommodating this might prove to you, that it is an ineluctable fact that credit is inextensible.

Secretary: Isn't there a simpler way of saying 'pay up'?

Then, the letter-writer who is a frustrated editor, who strikes *after* the letter is typed:

Businessman: Ah, that phrase should go there, now that really should go there – no I didn't mean denigrated – er, what's a better way of saying it … put down? No – stet. As you were – denigrated. And make it 'Yours sincerely' – 'Yours faithfully' is too formal. Can you get it done straight away?

Secretary: I'm afraid not sir, I've got all the other letters you re-wrote to type as well …

All a complete waste of time – the boss dictates, the secretary types, the boss rewrites, she retypes …

So, how should a good business letter be planned? It all boils down to two things – *work it out* and *keep it short*. Work out what you're going to say in advance, and make notes; then say it using short words, short sentences and short paragraphs. As closely as possible, stick to conventional language, not slang of course, but since you never say 'I feel it incumbent upon me as the recipient of your strictures', never *write* it either.

Now we have seen a few illustrations of *how* something ought to be expressed by letter, let's look at *what* is written in the good business letter. Imagine you have to write a letter to explain that an order of shirts from Japan won't be delivered to your customer because it has been held up at the docks …

Punctuation

Punctuation is a problem for many letter-writers – when to use commas, when not, and so on.

Many people make the mistake of inserting a comma, for example, when a pause seems necessary. This is the wrong approach. Although one of the purposes of punctuation is to supply the written word with the colour and emphasis that tone of voice, facial expression and gesture give to the spoken word, its main purpose is to enable the reader's mind to grasp the meaning of a phrase or sentence. Punctuation is an invaluable aid to clear writing.

So the rule is: punctuate for meaning. If you keep to short sentences, you will not need more than commas and full stops, with the occasional question mark.

Planning

The first thing to do is to think about the letter you intend to write, then compile the information you need, then make notes or write a rough draft of the letter you intend to send.

Clearly a letter asking for an overdraft won't need as much thinking about as some others, but 'Dear Sir, I need more money. Yours sincerely,' is not sufficient.

Writing down your thoughts on the letter you are about to write and then putting these thoughts in order (using the SCRAP method) will highlight what must be said and what needn't be said.

It cannot be repeated often enough that the main, indeed the only, purpose of a business letter is to get results – i.e. the information or action you want.

Dear Sirs,

Re your esteemed favour of the 15th inst., I can offer you instead another line or two, one being more pricey than the other, as the shipment is held up at the docks by an Act of God. We're terribly sorry about this but we're both in the same boat. If we can't get the stuff, we can't get it to you owing to this cock-up at the docks. However, if you would like us to proceed with either Sylvester or Zabaglione items, as per catalogue in place of your Yamoko order, we would be pleased to proceed forthwith. Awaiting the favour of your esteemed command and assuring you of our best attention at all times,

I remain, yours sincerely.

That's *all* wrong; in tone and content. Some of the faults we have already looked at – archaic Dickensian phrases, alternating with slang, 'Act of God' when what is meant is 'the Customs' and so on. But it is also wrong in simple construction. Remember a useful mnemonic: SCRAP, standing for Situation, Complication, Resolution, Action, Politeness. It will help you in many, many letters. The Situation is a statement of the fact or facts with which the letter is concerned; the Complication develops the facts and suggests a problem or asks a question; the Resolution suggests a solution; Action is a simple statement of alternatives – we know how we would like to proceed, in which case we will do such and such, but if this is unacceptable, then such and such will happen; Politeness is self-explanatory.

In the example above, the Situation is that an order has been received and it hasn't arrived. The Complication is that the order is held up at the docks and the letter-writer doesn't know when it will be released; the Resolution is to offer what is available – other brands which have not been ordered; Action is a statement of the alternatives – will the customer wait for his order to be released or accept an alternative supply? Politeness, in this case, means making the letter more *personal*, and expressing fellow-feeling and goodwill.

	Dear Mr Parker,
	Yamoko Sports Shirts
Situation	I'm sorry we cannot deliver the Yamoko Sports Shirts you ordered on 15 January.
Complication	The department of Customs and Excise tell us that that shipment has been held up at the docks. They do not know when it will be released.
	As an alternative we can supply:
Resolution	1. the locally-made Sylvester shirts at £206 per dozen, immediate delivery. 2. the Italian-made Zabaglione sports shirts at £244 per dozen, delivery within forty-eight hours. Both Sylvester and Zabaglione are good value. They are available in a wide range of colours and sizes, and compare well with Yamoko sports shirts. I enclose our catalogue. Pages 15–17 will give you all the necessary information.
Action	I will telephone early next week to find out which alternative you prefer.
Politeness	All good wishes, yours sincerely,

SCRAP

S.C.R.A.P. It's worth underlining the importance of the mnemonic (or 'aid to the memory') SCRAP. The letters stand for –

Situation
Complication
Resolution
Action
Politeness

– and indicate the order in which a business letter should be laid out.

Which of the letters would you prefer to have written? Which would you prefer to have *received*? Thinking of the latter is often a good guide to the former.

Letter layout

1 Follow the house rules on letter layout. For instance, whether or not to indent paragraphs, use reference numbers, reference initials, etc.

2 Check and follow any house rules on spelling, abbreviations, hyphenating words, letter endings, use of job titles, etc.

3 If no house rules exist, use the following guidelines:
a: indent paragraphs if you have a company letterhead which is centred on the page. Letter endings, i.e. name and job title, should then be centred.
b: range all copy to a straight left-hand margin if you have a letterhead which is 'ranged left'. Letter endings, i.e. name and job title, should then be ranged left.

c: only hyphenate or break words where the hyphenation is natural or the break makes sense as two separate words/ syllables on different lines, e.g. dis-similar, dis-jointed, sub-terranean.

4 Letters should be signed by an individual with the individual's name and job title clearly typed beneath the signature. Not:
a: per pro the XYZ organization
b: for and on behalf of

The correct endings are as follows:

Yours sincerely

John Coates
Manager, Planning Development

Yours faithfully,

Sebastian Pound
Customer Accounts Supervisor

Sample letters

Sales Letter– Direct Mail

Mr Frank N. Stein
Temples of Rest Ltd
Gravesend
Kent

Dear Mr Stein,

As a frequent organizer of conferences and meetings, you will be interested to hear about the Hades Hotel which has recently been extended to include a seminar suite.

We know that finding exactly the right facilities at the right price can present problems and believe we may now be able to help you solve them.

Situated only a few minutes' drive from Gravesend, the Hades Hotel can now offer a wide variety of meeting rooms to suit all requirements. The facilities are described in detail in the enclosed brochure. But why not come and see them for yourself?

My secretary will telephone you to arrange a convenient time. All our staff look forward to giving you a warm welcome.

I look forward to meeting you.

Yours sincerely,

Hilary James
Banqueting Manager

Miss J Evans
43 Doncaster Road
Sheffield
South Yorkshire

Dear Miss Evans,

Thank you for your recent order for the suit
advertised in our autumn catalogue.

This style, in the colour you requested, has
proved to be very popular. I very much regret
that we have sold our complete stock.

May I suggest that you look at the enclosed leaflet
of new additions to our autumn range, several of
which are available in the colour of your choice
and at the same price? The style you requested
is still available in navy blue and moss green.

Please mark your new selection on the enclosed
form. Alternatively you may request a cash
refund which will be sent to you by return.

I look forward to hearing from you.

Yours sincerely,

Valerie Pike
Sales Department

Sales Letter – Follow Up

Dear Pleasure Seeker,

Summer is nearly here and the evenings are getting
longer. But when the summer is over, how will
you store your garden furniture?

Manufacturers have at last realized that storage
of garden furniture - when not in use in summer
and during winter storage - is a problem for many
people.

Many types of folding or knock-down furniture have
now appeared on the market but we believe we have
produced the ultimate answer.

Our new Awayday armchair is the best in foldability.
It has four aluminium legs and one of the back
uprights is shaped like an umbrella handle. Folded,
the chair is like a flat umbrella, only five inches
in diameter. It weighs less than 4 lbs. Opened
in a second, it becomes a chair with a seat, back
and armrests, all made of brightly striped nylon
material in a choice of colours.

The demand for Awayday is likely to be overwhelming.
We are, therefore, offering you the chance to order
yours now. Just complete and return the reply paid
coupon with your payment and your chairs will be
with you within 28 days.

Best wishes for a wonderful summer!

Yours faithfully,

Letter of Complaint

Dear Sirs,

<u>5 Cedar Grove</u>

I wrote to you on 10 August regarding a leak
from the bathroom of the first-floor flat in
this property.   The leak has caused considerable
damage to the decorations of the ground-floor flat.

I have not yet received a reply to my letter and
the state of the decorations in the ground-floor
flat is deteriorating rapidly.

As this appears to be a structural defect for
which the residents in the block have communal
responsibility, I believe it is your role, as
managing agents, to see that it is put right.

I should be grateful, therefore, if you would
arrange for the leak to be repaired within the
next three days.   Otherwise I shall have to take
legal action.

Thank you for your help.   I look forward to a
successful resolution of this matter.

Yours faithfully,

Answer
to a complaint

Miss Mona Lot
3 St George's Drive
Blank Town
Hampshire

Dear Miss Lot,

Thank you for telling us you have received an
incorrect statement of account.

I regret that, although I have checked very
thoroughly, I can find no trace of your payment.

May I suggest that you contact your bank to see
whether your cheque has been cleared?   If the
cheque has been cleared, I would be most grateful
if you would tell me the date of payment from
your bank and supply our batch number details.
These details will have been stamped on the back
of your cheque.

Assuming no clearance has been made, you would
be advised to stop your cheque and supply us with
a new cheque to clear your account.

Thank you for your help.

Yours sincerely,

Helen Watts
Customer Liaison Department

Dear Mrs Sparks,

Thank you for your telephone enquiry about British schools in Japan.

I regret that the Japanese Embassy are unable to help in this respect.   I can only suggest that you write, giving full details of your requirements, to the British Embassy in Tokyo.   The address of the British Embassy is ...

I am enclosing some information on the Japanese education system which will tell you more about our educational and cultural heritage.

I hope that you find a satisfactory solution to your problem and enjoy your stay in Japan.

Yours sincerely,

Confirmation

Channel Crossing Ltd
Ramsgate
Kent

Dear Sirs,

Ref: SO41063

I telephoned you this morning to make a reservation for two passengers with car travelling between Dover and Boulogne.

Our arrangements have now changed.   I wish to confirm the outward journey from Dover to Boulogne on Flight no.731 on Monday 13 September 1982, but wish to cancel the return journey from Boulogne to Dover on Monday 27 September.

I enclose my cheque for £52.00 together with a completed booking form.   I look forward to receiving confirmation and the tickets soon.

Thank you for your help.

Yours faithfully,

Debt Chasing

Dear Mr Applegate,

It appears that we have not yet received payment of our invoice, no. 9182, sent to you last December.

Our terms of business - stated on all our estimates and invoices - are 30 days net. Your invoice has now been outstanding for 90 days.   It is our company policy to take legal action on all outstanding debts of this duration.

To avoid this embarrassing situation, would you please send us a cheque by return.   I am enclosing a copy of our invoice in case the original has gone astray.

I look forward to receiving your payment by return.

Yours sincerely,

Job Turn-Down

Dear Ms Brown,

Administrative Assistant to the Managing Director

Thank you for coming to see me last week in connection with your application for this position.

I have now interviewed all the candidates on our short-list and regret that on this occasion your application was not successful.

There is another vacancy in the company for which I feel you may well be suited and I am enclosing details.

If this new vacancy is of interest, please ring me by Friday 14 June to arrange an appointment.

I look forward to hearing from you.

Yours sincerely,

Dorren Phillips
Personnel Manager

Golden rules

Business letters are a permanent record.

Avoid trade jargon unless you are corresponding with someone who will know it.

Clarity, simplicity and brevity are the hallmarks of a good business letter.

Think of the reactions of the recipient of the letter.

Plan the more difficult letters before you dictate them.

Use the SCRAP method.

Think of the reactions of the recipient of the letter.

Nobody ever admits to being a bad driver, a bad lover or a bad interviewer. Most bad interviewers think that they are rather good. There are two principal reasons for this delusion. One is that interviewing a candidate sets the interviewer in a position of power and patronage which is a rare delight to the ego and a temptation to self-indulgence. It is hard to be self-critical in a position when you are assessing somebody else. The other reason is the absence of any

6 Manhunt — the selection interview

... to paraphrase Napoleon, every clerk carries a personalized number plate in his briefcase ...

Interviewing sets the interviewer in a position of power and patronage which is a rare delight to the ego and a temptation to self-indulgence.

obvious criteria which would make the interviewer concede that he had done his job badly. For example, if he misses the best candidate he is unlikely ever to discover his mistake; and if he picks the wrong one he will have a string of plausible reasons for the person's failure before he even has to consider the possibility that if he had interviewed him properly he would never have given him the job in the first place.

Although it is hard to pin down responsibility, the fact is that companies can easily be victims of poor selection. Bad recruitment may lead to any number of problems, including a high turnover of staff. Take Tom Harding's company, facing yet another resignation. Harding's assistant, Davenport, rushes in with the news:

The administrative disciplines

The job specification

The candidate must be supplied – well before the interview – with a description of the job, including all relevant details. This gives him a chance to withdraw if, e.g., it requires him to spend three months a year in Calcutta and he can't stand heat. A full job specification saves much uncertainty, confusion and time-wasting.

In addition to the job specification sheet you should also prepare a 'man profile' – a guide to the sort of age, background, experience and qualifications you are looking for and not looking for. This is for internal use and not for the candidate.

It can also be helpful to supply candidates with a brief booklet – if you have one –

Davenport: Costello's leaving!

Harding: I know. Ivan phoned me.

Davenport: That's five. Five new managers in seven months. Tom, I don't understand what's going wrong.

Harding: I do. At least, I think I do. Go through the reasons why they've left.

Davenport: Well, Costello says he wants to move towards actuarial work, not line management. Francis's wife couldn't find any work here and got bored at home. Young Stanton wasn't up to it technically and Baker turns out never to have run a group in his life. As for Morrison, he was a professional job-hopper …

Harding: Exactly, and you've just explained the problem. None of them suddenly changed his life-style. They were all bad risks when they joined us. And we should have found that out before we recruited them.

The selection interview is a manhunt. It should be a piece of detective work, in which every available clue is used – the only difference is that in this instance the interviewers are looking for a good man instead of a bad one. The skills are the same. They are skills you have to learn if you are to get your man, or woman.

There are three principal reasons why so many good managers make bad interviewers: they do not use their eyes, they do not use their ears, and they do not use their tongues.

Let's take the eyes first. Bad interviewers don't study the application form, they don't study the job specification, half the time they don't even look in their own diary to make sure that they are not going to be interrupted during the interview. Ethelred the Unready, who is one of Tom Harding's managers, is a prime example of this type of interviewer:

Ethelred: Well now, hello Mr …

The telephone rings, and of course he picks it up.

Ethelred: Oh, Jack, we're up 34 per cent on budget and ahead of the last quarter. Is that what you want? OK. Sorry about that, Mr … Hibbitt?

Arnold: No. Mr Arnold.

Ethelred: Arnold, of course. Lorna, have they sent across Mr Arnold's application form yet?

Lorna: It's in your tray, sir.

Ethelred: Ah, yes. Thank you very much for coming along, Mr Arnold. I thought we'd just have a chat about … well, anything that occurs … Now, which job is this for? I don't seem to have the right papers …

Arnold: It's the Assistant Budgets Officer.

Ethelred: Right … Well, your application looks the sort of thing. What do you want to know?

Arnold: Would I be doing sales as well as expense budgets?

Ethelred: Er … Well, now. We had a meeting about that. What did we decide? … I should have looked it up. Anything else I can clear up for you? No? You really want this job, do you? The point of it is to get the whole … no, let me tell you about the company first. We …

So the first skill of a selection detective is to use his eyes. Look for clues in the application form, look ahead to forestall interruptions, and look ahead to anticipate any questions the candidate might ask.

Because of his concern at the company's bad record for recruitment, Tom Harding has decided to second-interview all the candidates himself. Let's see how he copes with Mr Arnold:

describing the company and its activities.

The application form

Apart from screening out the obviously unsuitable candidate, this saves a whole lot of time-wasting at the interview, and also gives the interviewer valuable preliminary guidance for his line of questioning.

Preparation

Of course the interviewer must be flexible and prepared to follow up unforeseen points that crop up during the interview. Nevertheless, he should have prepared certain questions to which he must find the answers during the interview. These will normally fall into two categories:

a: Job-centred questions: questions prompted by the special requirements of the job. These will be questions to ask all the candidates.

b: Man-centred questions: questions prompted by the application form, e.g. at points where the interviewer suspects the man may not be right for the job. These questions will vary from candidate to candidate.

Follow-up

As soon as the candidate leaves the room it is essential to write notes and a summary of your conclusions. This does not matter so much if you only do one interview a quarter, but if you do several in a day it is vital, or you will forget all about some candidates. If the candidate is not suitable for this job but might be happy and valuable in a different job in the company, 'follow-up' includes taking action on this.

Structure the interview

The reason for a formal structure is to make sure you do not miss anything. You and the candidate are only together for a limited time, and it is difficult, wasteful and inefficient to recall him because of something you forgot to ask. You want to make sure that when he goes out of the door you have discovered all you can to enable you to make up your mind. If you follow a planned pattern of questioning you are likely to achieve this. If you dart to and fro you are much more likely to miss an important area.

a: The seven-point plan:*
   i: Physical make-up
   ii: Attainments
   iii: General intelligence
   iv: Special aptitudes
   v: Interests
   vi: Disposition
   vii: Personal circumstances

Secretary: Mr Arnold's just arrived.

Harding: Thank you. May I have the job description, Mr Arnold's application and my notes – and will you take all my phone calls for the next half hour, please? Mr Arnold, do come in. My name's Tom Harding. Divisional Director. What I'd like to do is to outline very briefly the structure of our meeting. First of all I'd like to answer any questions you may have, and then if you're satisfied I'd like to find out a bit more about you.

So. Have you any basic points you'd like cleared up?

Arnold: Would I be doing sales as well as expense budgets?

Harding: Yes, to ensure that they're properly linked.

Arnold: And what sort of computer have you got?

Harding: The 1902A ... tape and disc configuration. Have you had much computer experience?

Arnold: I've had some. One of our major clients has a 360.

Harding: Good. Any other queries about the job? Right, we'll carry on. How do you feel about moving out of a Head Office environment and coming into one that's clearly an operational unit?

Arnold: I'm very happy about it. I want to get some experience at the sharp end.

Harding: You'd have to move here. Have you thought about your wife getting a job? I don't know whether there's much demand for remedial teachers.

Arnold: Most larger schools seem to have them now. I can't see that becoming a problem ...

The second cause of bad interviewing is not listening – not giving the candidate a

chance to relax and expand, forever inter-
rupting, answering your own questions, and
pontificating. It's all too easy to make the
interviewee retreat into his shell. That's the
speciality of Ivan the Terrible, another of Mr
Harding's managers:

Brand: John Brand, sir.

Ivan: So. You didn't finish technical
college?

Brand: No, I decided that ...

Ivan: Read the *Guardian*, do you? Now,
about the job. I run the department and
I'm glad to say it's the fastest-growing
department in the company. And that's
not bad in this company, I can tell you.
Anything else?

Brand: I was just going to explain ...

Ivan: What are your 'A' levels?

Brand: Maths and physics.

Ivan: Ever been a boss?

Brand: No.

Ivan: Well in this job you'd have seven
under you.

Brand: Oh, I've supervised people before.
At Tetherton's I've got five people ...

Ivan: But you just said you hadn't.

Brand: I didn't think of myself as a
boss ...

Ivan: Well a boss is a boss. Five?

Brand: Yes, I supervise two on sales
invoicing, two on stock records and one
typist.

Ivan: You don't count typists. You don't
have the look of a boss. You know why?
You haven't got boss eyes. Don't look
so worried! It's only a joke. Just creating
rapport, trying to put you at your ease.
Relax! ... Is your wife on the pill?

Brand: What?

Ivan: Are you going to have kids?

Brand: Not for two or three years, no.

Ivan: Why not?

Brand: She enjoys her job very much and

b: The five point plan:†
  i: Impact on others
  ii: Qualifications
  iii: Innate abilities
  iv: Motivation
  v: Adjustment

c: The three areas the
candidate must talk on:‡
  i: The past: get him
    talking about his
    previous job, early life,
    etc.
  ii: The present: elicit his
    current views,
    attitudes, opinions
    and judgements.
  iii: The future: his aims,
    ambitions, long-term
    career objectives, the
    sort of life he wants to
    lead.

If the job has special
technical requirements, his
ability and experience must be
thoroughly explored to test
their breadth and depth. If you
are not capable of doing this
yourself, you would be wise to
ask a technically expert
colleague to have a separate
talk with the candidate and
give you a professional
assessment.

There are other plans too,
but as you see they are all
different ways of slicing the
same cake. The important
thing is to follow a plan. Which
plan you follow is much less
significant.

* Professor Alec Rodger,
National Institute of Industrial
Psychology
† J. Munro Fraser
‡ Romney Rawes, Reed
Executive Selection

we feel we don't want to start a family yet.

Ivan: A bit women's lib, is she? I see. What do you think about all that, then? I mean, I've got nothing against it, but it's the problems it brings with kids. I like to find out about a chap's family, get some picture of what his home life's like. It tells you more about a chap than all these forms ... I don't go for all that, I'm afraid. I pick the chap, not his qualifications. It's my proud boast that I've not picked a wrong one yet and I've been doing it nearly fifteen years. Now, should invoices be approved by buying or accounts?

Brand: Well, I've changed my mind about this. I used ...

Ivan: It's got to be accounts, hasn't it? These buying fellows'll pass anything. What are the qualities of a good manager?

Brand: I've thought about this, and I'm not sure it isn't to do with being helpful ...

Ivan: Well, they're supposed to help you, aren't they? I mean you're the boss. Its the old delegation problem. Sometimes I think that's the hardest problem of all – knowing when to delegate. I mean, you've got to give people a chance, haven't you? I've always followed a policy of delegation and it's worked for me. You'll find a lot of chaps dotted around this company who got their first taste of responsibility here ...

The second skill of the selection detective is to get the candidate talking, then listen to what he's saying and how he's saying it. Did Ivan discover *anything* about Mr Brand? Let's see how Tom Harding interviewed the same candidate:

Brand: ... as I tried to tell the other gentleman, that's why I left technical college early.

Harding: Well, I think that covers most of the points. There's one thing we haven't touched on, though. If you were to come here you'd have seven people working under you. From your experience at Tetherton's, what do you think are the essential qualities of a good manager?

Brand: I have the feeling that it's to do with helpfulness ... making people in the group feel that you are there to help them. If they've got problems, you really want to know what they are and help to chew them over.

Harding: How about the old problem of them bringing you things they ought to be able to sort out themselves?

Brand: Well, if they do that, you've got to help them to establish what's referable. But provided you encourage them to help themselves, there's no reason why they should be lazy about their responsibilities.

Harding: And that doesn't mean they tend to take up too much of your time?

Brand: If the problem is difficult, it should take up my time, or a good part of it.

Harding: How formal are your relations with the people under you?

Brand: Very informal. Christian name terms, apart from one chap I'm a bit more formal with because it seems to work better that way.

Harding: Does this informality make it more difficult to sack people?

Brand: I've never given anyone the sack. I was once told to, but I refused. The next week he offered his resignation.

Harding: So that solved that?

Brand: Oh, I didn't accept it. But it

The courtesies

1 The candidate should have date and time confirmed on paper, with clear directions how to get to you.
2 The receptionist should have the candidate's name so that he knows he is expected.
3 There should be a mirror in the waiting room or outer office.
4 The interview should start punctually.
5 The interviewer should stand up, shake hands, show the candidate where to hang his hat and coat and offer him a chair.
6 The interviewer should have the application form in front of him and make it clear he has read it and thought about it.
7 There should, if possible, be a clock on the wall easily visible to the interviewer, so that he does not have to keep glancing at his watch.
8 It should be made quite clear when the interview is over, and what the next stage will be, e.g. short-list, letter within two weeks, second interview etc.
9 If it is likely that the candidate will be unsuccessful, he should be given some hint of this, e.g., 'I've got a feeling this isn't the job for you'. If it is certain he has not got the

job, he should be told so there and then.

10 If it is likely the candidate will be successful, this should be hinted too – 'Clearly your application will have to be taken very seriously'.

11 If the candidate, though wrong for the job, is a good man, he should be asked if he would be interested in a different job if one came up.

12 The secretary or receptionist should get a note of the candidate's expenses before he leaves.

13 He should leave feeling that he has had a civilized and stimulating conversation which gave him every opportunity to put his case and provided his interviewer with all the data he would wish him to have in order to make a fair decision.

14 The decision should be made promptly and notified swiftly.

meant we were able to talk things over, in a way we could never have done otherwise, and we sorted it out. That's the chap I'm a bit more formal with now. It works better that way, I don't exactly know why.

Harding: Fine. Well that's all I wanted to ask you. Is there anything you'd like to say that you haven't had a chance to?

Brand: I don't think so.

Harding: Well you've clearly had some very relevant experience. Thank you for coming to see me. I hope to be able to let you know one way or the other by the weekend. Please don't forget to give my secretary a note of your expenses before you go.

The third mistake made by bad interviewers is not speaking out – failing to direct the interview down the line you want to follow; failing to follow up clues by keeping your doubts and suspicions to yourself instead of putting them frankly to the candidate. That's the mark of another of Harding's managers, William the Silent:

Colville: ... of course it's very

I've got a feeling this isn't the job for you, Mr Scrutton ...

commercialized now, but when we first went there it was delightful. So we go to Lanzarelli up in the north-east now, only an hour away, but still untouched. Bit hot in July and August, but I'd recommend it ... sorry, I seem to be chatting on ...

William: Not at all.

Colville: Please, do ...

William: Well, perhaps just a few questions ... I see that you went to the Geneva International Management Centre for twelve months. Got the diploma?

Colville: Yes.

William: Diploma ... I do love the lake there in Geneva. Then you joined Universal International as a trainee ...

Colville: Yes, I wanted to get a really thorough training.

William: And after sixteen months in the marketing department you didn't start the next job for nine months ...

Colville: I was determined to wait for the right job.

William: Very wise. So in those nine months you ... didn't do anything in particular?

Colville: No.

William: Nothing ... in ... particular. Well, we all do a bit of that ... splendid. Then three years as PA to the Marketing Director at Parker and Gibbs?

Colville: Then they asked me to start a Management Services Section.

William: Yes ... er ... one tiny thing. You put it on its feet, and ran it for eleven months and then it was ... er ...

Colville: Decentralized.

William: Ah yes. Exactly. Decentralized. Could I ask why it ... er ...

Colville: The reason they decentralized

The technique

The interview obviously has only one purpose – to pick the right man or woman for the job. But there are two ways of failing to achieve this objective.

i: By picking the wrong candidate: that is, by failing to expose qualifications which good questioning would have revealed.

ii: By missing the right candidate: that is, by failing to draw out facts, attitudes, experience and personal qualities which good interviewing would have elicited.

Not picking the wrong candidate. Occasionally this is spectacular, e.g. questioning about a twelve-month job-gap which the candidate said was spent straightening out his wife's business but which on closer enquiry turned out to have been passed in Wormwood Scrubs for embezzlement. Less spectacular 'wrong' candidates

was that it had served its purpose. We'd shown people how to get the information themselves, so our job was done and we were able to let people get on with it for themselves.

William: Quite, so then you went back to being PA to the Sales Manager ... till three months ago. As Sales Manager of the north-east region here you'd have about forty men under you.

Colville: There were twenty in the Marketing Department at Parker and Gibbs.

William: So you've had plenty of experience of dealing with chaps ... Of course, up in the north-east they can be a bit ... blunt, in a manner of speaking.

Colville: That's what I like about them. No beating about the bush. They come straight out with things.

William: Absolutely. I can't stand all this ...

Colville: Beating about the bush.

The third skill, then, is using your own tongue. Questioning, probing, putting your doubts and suspicions frankly to the candidate is fundamental. After all, it's the only way he'll get a chance to answer them.

When Tom Harding interviewed Colville he delved a little deeper into the applicant's past than William the Silent had done:

Harding: I understand most of what you've told me, but I'd like to clear up a few points. What subjects did this diploma at the Geneva Management Centre cover?

Colville: French.

Harding: Just French?

Colville: It was a tough course to obtain fluency.

Harding: Was there an exam for the diploma?

Colville: Not as such.

Harding: So it was an attendance certificate.

Colville: In a way. But it was a tough course.

Harding: Now after sixteen months with Universal there was a nine-month gap before you joined Parker and Gibbs.

Colville: I felt that I was at a crossroads, and that it was very important to take time and wait until the right thing came along.

Harding: Nine months is a long time if you're really set on a marketing career. How many jobs did you apply for during this period?

Colville: Quite a lot.

Harding: Ten? Forty?

Colville: About ten.

Harding: Round about one a month. Now at Parker and Gibbs there were about twenty people in the Marketing Department?

Colville: That's right.

Harding: How many were you directly responsible for?

Colville: Two. My PA and a typist. That's all we needed really. It wasn't a job that required much … clerical staff.

Harding: Quite. Now, when this Management Services Section closed down … it must have been a bit of a set-back for you?

Colville: Not really. We'd accomplished our aim.

Harding: But surely it wasn't set up with the intention of closing it down so quickly?

Colville: Not entirely, no. It was a kind of experiment.

Harding: And from the company's point of view it was a failure.

Colville: They never really gave it a chance.

are the spy from a rival company, the professional job-hopper, the man who lies about his age, salary or reason for leaving his last job, and the one just wanting the offer as a lever to use on his present employer. But more often it is a question or rigour and clarity about the job requirements. Qualifications and disqualifications emerge when the questioner is really thinking imaginatively about what the job will demand from the person in front of him.

Picking the right candidate.
If the right candidate is also a lively extrovert, it is usually not too hard to pick him. The skill comes in revealing the best man when he is quiet, unassuming and reserved.

This depends on creating an atmosphere and a situation in which he will talk in his most open manner. It is important to put him at ease, to relax the atmosphere and to find some common interest or experience that creates a personal rapport. The pitfall here is to do all the talking yourself: 40 per cent should be about the overall maximum for the interviewer, but it should be an average – higher at the start and decreasing as the interview progresses. Avoid questions that have 'yes' or 'no' answers unless you plan to follow them with an open one, e.g. 'why?' or 'why not?'.

Harding: So you went back to Marketing
as PA to the Sales Manager. But before
that you were PA to the Marketing
Director. So this was demotion?

Colville: Not at all. It was a sideways
move to gain experience nearer to the
grassroots.

Harding: But you took a drop in salary?

Colville: A slight one, technically. But
with my background I felt that I needed
this kind of experience before I could
command a substantially higher
salary.

Harding: Let me ask you a very direct
question. If you were interviewing a
chap who had left a successful firm
after sixteen months, had spent nine
months having one interview a month,
had then been put in charge of setting
up a section which was closed down in
under a year, had gone back to his old
department at a reduced salary ...
would you really be able to put him in
charge of forty bloody-minded
Geordies?

Colville: If you look at it like that ...

Harding: Unfortunately that's the way I
have to look at it, unless you can show
me I'm wrong.

Harding's problems are threefold: his
three managers. He follows up his own interviews by seeing Ethelred, Ivan and William
in turn. He talks with Ethelred:

Harding: Let's talk about the candidates,
beginning with Frank Arnold. Which
did you consider first – qualifications,
experience, or personality?

Ethelred: Yes. I mean I do them all first,
really ... play it by ear.

Harding: Let's look at it another way.
What sort of a fellow do you think we're
looking for?

Ethelred: Good point. Let's start with that.

Harding: Then we can work out what questions to ask them.

Ethelred: Right. What?

Harding: So we don't miss anything important.

And Ivan:

Ivan: That bloke Shelley's the one. Spotted him right away. Better get on to Personnel and offer him the job.

Harding: But he's on £6,900 at the moment ... top of the scale for this is £5,600.

Ivan: Are you sure? £6,900?

Harding: He said he'd told you. What do you think of Brand?

Ivan: Didn't come over as strong as Shelley. Didn't have much to say for himself. I didn't get much of an impression of him ...

And William:

William: Well I'm damned. He took me in. How did you find all this out?

Harding: I asked him.

William: Just as well you did.

Harding has a lot to teach his managers before they will begin to make progress. Any amateur interviewer can get a fair personal impression of a candidate. But the professional does something else as well: he compiles a dossier of factual evidence. He does this by preparing, communicating and probing.

1 **Preparing.** The professional has produced and supplied to the candidate a clear and detailed job specification. He has studied the application form and checked on the candidate's

111

qualifications. He has worked out a plan of areas to cover and questions to ask. He has cleared out his diary and given instructions to his secretary and the switchboard that he is not to be interrupted.

2 **Communicating**. The professional finds ways of making the candidate feel easy and relaxed, and gets him talking freely, openly and relevantly.

3 **Probing**. The professional has worked out in advance the particular answers he needs to find out during the interview, the doubts and suspicions he wants cleared up, the ambiguities and contradictions he wants resolved. He is constantly alert for any further clues that may suggest the candidate is particularly suitable, or particularly unsuitable, for this specific job. He has prepared a path that he intends to follow, though he is prepared to depart from it at any instant if a significant point crops up.

*....Dear Lord,
Let there be some doubt ...*

A final point to bear in mind: there are two aspects to an interview, one irrational and one rational. The irrational part is the feeling you have about a candidate. If he is going to work for you, and your instinct tells you that you are not going to get on with him, you will almost certainly be right to follow your instinct. Most people do this, and because they are unlikely to be wrong, it forms the delusion that they 'know how to pick 'em'. But most of the time there is no such clear feeling, and it is then that the rational element comes in. It is a question of determining which of the candidates has the necessary background, qualifications, experience, attitudes and temperament to do the job that has to be done. These are uncharted waters for the likes of Ethelred, Ivan and William ...

Golden rules

Read the application form and anticipate questions you might be asked.

Use a planned pattern for questioning.

Don't just talk, listen. At least 60 per cent of the words exchanged should be the interviewee's, not the interviewer's.

Don't keep doubts to yourself – come out with them.

Use open questions.

When in doubt, follow your 'irrational' instincts.

Write notes and conclusions after each interview.

Do you, as a manager, keep your staff in the dark about their performance? Do they know what *you* think of them? As an employee, does your boss find time to tell you how he feels about your work – does he *know* about it, your most important achievements, or failures? Many companies have an annual appraisal interview designed specifically for this purpose. Unfortunately they can turn out to be worse than useless. Take the experiences of Alan Ames, who has had the misfortune to work for each of those three enemies of society, Ethelred the Unready, Ivan the Terrible and William the Silent. It all comes back to him during another annual event – his regular medical check-up …

Dr Evans: Nice to see you again, Alan. How are you?

Ames: Fine.

Dr Evans: Good. Sit down. I'm all for these annual get-togethers; if there's anything slightly wrong, we can nip it in the bud. So … how are things?

Ames: Great. I left that company, Parks and Gibb. I'm with a new firm.

Dr Evans: Same sort of work?

Ames: Yes, but it's like being in the daylight after five years in the dark. I know what I have to do; I know where I fit in. I mean, when I think back to that lot … Nobody ever listened to you, nobody told you what you had to do. You felt so helpless. The good people left because there wasn't enough in their jobs to keep them there, and the bad people stayed put because nobody found them out. I mean, you'd think it was in *their* interest to get the *best* out of people, wouldn't you? Give 'em work they can do and enjoy, or train 'em if they can't. I mean, that's the bloody *problem*!!!

Dr Evans: Careful! I've got to take your

7 How am I doing? The appraisal interview

The employee's needs

What is expected?
How am I doing?
Where am I going?
What can I do to improve?

Based on these four questions, it is quickly apparent that your role is to appraise performance in the job, and this appraisal is conducted against the background of the job description, standards of performance and short-term priority tasks.

If your employee needs the answers to the four questions above, you also need the answers and his views to help you with your assessment. Remember, appraisal should be a dialogue.

The benefits of appraisal

Why should you, a manager, in daily or weekly contact with a member of your team, carry out an appraisal interview?

The benefits can really be divided into three headings:

To the individual
To you, the manager
To the organization

The individual

An employee likes and needs to know how he is getting on and to have an opportunity to discuss his work in detail to find out his boss's view of him and how he can work more effectively. He also needs to discuss his future within the organization and how he sees his career developing.

The manager

You will gain from closer and detailed contact with the individual his views on his work, his ideas on what he does well or could do better,

blood pressure in a moment.

Ames: Sorry, but it still gets to me.

Dr Evans: But why was it so bad?

Ames: Because you never got a chance to really talk to your boss about your job. Were you happy, was *he* happy, how were things going? As simple as that.

Dr Evans: But you saw each other every day.

Ames: Yes, but that's like those people in your waiting room. You've got a lot of them to see every day. Those are the daily running problems. You haven't got time to give every one of those a full medical check-up.

Dr Evans: No, but I can always arrange a special session like this.

Ames: Yes, *you* can. But we had those. Oh yes. The annual appraisal interviews. They were the salt in the wound. You went in raw, you came out bleeding. I can still remember one when I was in Sales under Ethelred. I'd really done jolly well that year. Worked flat out for weeks on a big overseas order. I was expecting a pat on the back …

Alan recalls the occasion bitterly:

Ethelred: Alan … Oh yes, annual interview.

Ames: Annual interview? I didn't know about this.

Ethelred: Yes, you remember. The Personnel Department in its wisdom decrees that we should have an annual interview.

Ames: When?

Ethelred: Well, I thought we could knock it off now.

Ames: Now?

Ethelred: Why not?

Ames: Well, I'd like to have done a bit of thinking …

Ethelred: Yes, well the only thing is I've

got a bit behind with them. I've got three this morning *and* lunch with the Chairman. Look, this is only a formality. I mean we see each other every day anyway. So … everything going OK?

Ames: Well, let's talk about it. Anywhere particular you'd like to start?

Ethelred: No. Nowhere in particular, no. No complaints. A pity about the mess-up over the relaunch of the PX 20. Still, you can't win 'em all.

Ames: But I wasn't working on the relaunch.

Ethelred: Weren't you? Well, never mind. Set us back three months that did.

Ames: Yes, but I had nothing to do with that.

Ethelred: No, right. Now. Been on any courses this year?

Ames: No.

Ethelred: Well, you should know. What about the new product range appreciation course, for instance?

Ames: Well, that was the course I asked to go on at this interview last year.

Ethelred: Oh did you? Oh well, good idea then. *Last* year's interview? I must take a look at that some time. Or of course there's a language course. But you don't speak any languages, do you?

Ames: Yes, I'm fairly fluent in French and German.

Ethelred: What?

Ames: It's on my file.

Ethelred: Yes, yes, I'm sure it is. Wish we'd known when the Frankfurt people were over here on the PX launch. Oh no, you weren't involved with that.

Ames: No! I wasn't.

Ethelred: I thought … Oh well, never mind. Now, we don't seem to be getting much general customer information from you.

his views on his future and what extra help he thinks he needs to be more effective.

The interview will also help you to discover, from the individual, areas of confusion or overlap in the job. And it will give you the opportunity to review performance over a long period (say, a year) as opposed to the 'snapshot' view that a five-minute discussion at the desk or on the shop-floor can give.

The organization

So how does the company gain? Appraisal properly conducted will create closer working relationships, highlight priorities, identify people with potential and throw up future training needs to meet either short-term or long-term priorities. It also helps to harness people's energies to the company.

Know what you're doing

At its simplest, an appraisal interview is a planned discussion between boss and subordinate to review how the subordinate has carried out his job since the last appraisal. This discussion is carried out with a number of set objectives in mind:

1 To review progress and priorities.
2 To resolve any problems in these areas.
3 To discuss the subordinate's future potential and future training needs.

At the end of the interview, the interviewee should know the answer to the question *'How Am I Doing?'*

Ames: Hell, I write up my report sheets.

Ethelred: No, I mean sort of general customer feedback for the marketing people.

Ames: Surely that's not my responsibility, is it?

Ethelred: Yes!

Ames: It wasn't in my job description.

Ethelred: Wasn't it? Well, I mean, you can't be *too* rigid about that. Personnel Department bumph. I mean you've got to take it with a pinch of salt. Anyway, the main thing is to make sure you do it in the future. OK?

Ames: Yes, but you've never mentioned that I hadn't been making them up before.

Ethelred: No. Well, I mean, that's what these annual interviews are for isn't it? Pick up the mistakes that haven't been mentioned during the year. Anything else? Oh, yes, you're nearly due for a salary review. We could knock that off too while you're here. Now, you'll be getting the general increase next month. OK?

Ames: Well, I wondered if I wasn't due a bit more than the ordinary rise.

Ethelred: Well, there are a lot of chaps older than you on the same scale, Alan.

Ames: You mean I'm not worth any more?

Ethelred: Alan, you know me. I'd double everyone's salary if I could …

Ames: Look, have you talked to Les Strudwick about my Iranian presentation?

Ethelred: Not as such, no.

Ames: It went very well.

Ethelred: Yes, well I agree he hasn't complained.

Ames: Complained! We got the order!

Ethelred: Yes. Well, as I said, Alan, generally I've got no complaint …

Ames: *No complaint!*

Ethelred: As far as I know, no.

Ames: What do you mean, you've got no complaint 'as far as you know'? I mean, how can we discuss a complaint if you don't know whether you've got one or not. Look, what about the Iranian order?

Ethelred: Yes, well. That was jolly good. Jolly good. You were on that … ?

Still seething, Alan catalogues Ethelred's failings for Dr Evans:

Ames: He just hadn't taken the trouble to find out the first thing about me. Didn't even tell me I was going to have an annual interview and give me time to think about it. Hadn't talked to the *export manager* about the work I'd done for him … didn't even have the record of my previous interview. Didn't have my job description. Hadn't looked at my personal file. Our one big chat of the year and he hadn't done five minutes homework on it. Just not interested. Typical of the whole bloody company …

Dr Evans: I was just thinking what it would be like if a doctor started behaving like that at a check-up. I mean, think of Ethelred as a doctor …

Ethelred: Ah, Mr Ames, do sit down.

Ames: Thank you.

Ethelred: Well, well, well. I haven't seen you since …

Ames: The operation.

Ethelred: What? No, no, no. I've seen you since then. That was two years ago.

Ames: No it wasn't.

Ethelred: Yes it was. I went straight in after I'd got back from Spain.

Ames: No, no – *my* operation.

Ethelred: Oh, *yours.* You've had an operation?

Prepare properly

1 Fix a mutually convenient time. Do it courteously – don't make it sound like a summons to an interrogation or devalue it by being too casual.
2 Don't fill the diary for the whole day with appraisal interviews. Remember that 'tail-end Charlie' will get short shrift, unfairly.
3 Describe to the interviewee, in advance, the format and procedure to help allay fears.
4 Give the interviewee a preparation document so that he can prepare too.
5 Read and review:
   a: job description
   b: standards of performance and priorities
   c: personal file
6 Review in advance any targets or special projects.
7 Consult peers whose departments interface with the work of the interviewee.
8 Prepare the interview room. That is, try to avoid

the 'desk barrier' but don't go too far and make it 'a pint at the pub'.

9 Ensure no interruptions.

10 Make sure any aggravation from a previous meeting is out of your system before starting the interview. It is not fair to have an important interview if *you* are below par.

Ames: Yes! Last month.

Ethelred: Ah. Did you ... enjoy it?

Ames: What?

Ethelred: How is it ... now?

Ames: ... Better.

Ethelred: Good, good, good. That's what we doctors are here for.

Ames: ... It was the heart transplant.

Ethelred: Mr Ames? ... Well, well, well, I was thinking it was Mr Adams ... and it was you. Well, I'd better take him off

Do I have to go back to the shopfloor?

Create an informal atmosphere.

your pills ... pronto. Well how are things ... in general, apart from ... the heart?

Ames: Fine. Not bad. I still get these headaches occasionally.

Ethelred: Well, we've got something that'll get rid of those immediately. Marvellous new stuff called Antiparacetin ...

Ames: Dr Marsh has just taken me off those.

Ethelred: Did he?

Ames: Yes, he said I had an aspirin allergy.

Ethelred: Ah, well. In that case best avoid

120

them.

Ames: Isn't this on my record? He said it could be fatal ... with the ...

Ethelred: ... the heart, yes, but only relatively fatal. Only in the strictly medical sense. Yes, ah, here's the card. Eyesight still OK?

Ames: Yes.

Ethelred: Good. Any after-effects from the hysterectomy?

Ames: What?

Ethelred: Hasn't it been depressing lately ...

Yes, that's exactly how Ethelred would approach his responsibilities to a patient. In fact there are a great many similarities between the good doctor and the good manager. People's careers are vital to them – so is their health. Both are worth a little homework on an occasion like the annual interview. Just as the doctor has to review the patient's case history in advance of the check-up, so the manager must do the same. In short he must know what he's talking about. Equally, however, he mustn't do *all* the talking. Alan recalls a memorable interview when he worked in Central Sales under Ivan ...

Ivan: Right. Well, as you know, this is the annual appraisal interview, where the company tells you what it thinks of you. There's your assessment ... plenty of room for improvement, as I think you'll agree.

Ames: Look, I'm sorry. I don't really understand this. What's this BB– for efficiency? How do you calculate this sort of thing?

Ivan: I don't have to calculate. I know.

Ames: Yes. But I ...

Ivan: You fly by the seat of your pants, Alan. You've got good instincts – but

The employee's expectations

An employee usually expects an opportunity to state his views on his work. He expects to be praised for work well done and, to the surprise of many managers, will frequently criticise his own performance when below par – well in advance of any comment by his boss. (Frequently, the interviewee will be harder on himself than the manager would have been.) Having said that, the interviewee respects the manager who points out and helps him with areas which are below par.

His expectations will include being given a fair hearing – he is not in court hearing a verdict. He will therefore expect to be able to discuss his views, his progress, future and training and to be able to disagree with any comments made and state the reasons for his disagreement.

He will also expect to voice his views on factors that may have impeded his progress. You, the boss, may be one of those factors; you may have to take the remarks, if fair, on the chin. Likewise, he will expect to be able to put forward and discuss his views on progress and the future, not just of himself, but of his department and the work itself as well as listening to and discussing your views.

Achieve a discussion

In classic interview style you would be well advised to get the conversation going with open-ended questions. These are questions which avoid 'yes' or 'no' answers and help to promote conversation. By creating a conversational atmosphere, you will help your employee to relax. This will aid a freer exchange of views, opinions and facts. Your open-ended questions should be directed to obtain facts and opinions from the employee on how he has seen his job and his performance in the job over the last year. Also to ascertain how he sees the future. Use questions like:

• What was the most

when it comes down to the detail, you won't get down to it.

Ames: But there are several other things …

Ivan: I know your sort, Alan. I've had plenty of experience of them …

Ames: Yes, but I don't accept that I'm inefficient.

Ivan: I'm telling you you are inefficient.

Ames: Well, where's your evidence?

Ivan: Evidence? Come on Alan … You don't like criticism, that's your trouble.

Ames: Look, if you mean the order office …

Ivan: Yes I do. It's a mess.

Ames: It's the way it's organized. Look, I've written out a new procedure.

Ivan: I hardly think this is the time …

Ames: But you're usually very busy, it's terribly difficult to get to see you.

Ivan: Well, I'm a busy man. I have to run a department that's responsible for …

Ames: Exactly. But *now* we've got some time together … I mean this new procedure is absolutely central to my job. This is what I'm supervising. At the moment we send out first an order acknowledgement, then an invoice, then a statement. Some customers pay on invoice, some pay on statement. Some even pay twice. The girls are bogged down in paper and they spend ages reconciling cheques and statements. What I suggest is that for all normal orders we send out just one document instead of three – a combined invoice and statement.

Ivan: Look, Alan, this is just proving my point, you can't take criticism.

Ames: I *can* take criticism.

Ivan: No you can't. I'm criticising you now, aren't I? And you're arguing. You're obstinate. You have to blame it all on someone else – it's the system.

It's the company, you'll be saying next.

Ames: I am not blaming the company. I was merely trying to improve the way we do things.

Ivan: Right. And I'm trying to improve the way *you* do things, Alan. You're so bloody busy telling everyone else where they're going wrong, you never stop and look at your own faults. Well that's what this interview is *for* ...

Finishing his recollection of this unhappy episode, Alan turns to Dr Evans:

Ames: See what I mean? You couldn't get through. There was no discussion of *facts* ...

Dr Evans: Yes, I can imagine Ivan as a doctor ...

...

Ivan: You've got a nasty pain there.

Ames: Where?

Ivan: There.

Ames: ... No I haven't.

Ivan: Nasty pain.

Ames: Really I *haven't* got a pain there.

Ivan: Now, now. *Who's* the doctor? Have you got medical qualifications? No? Right. On the scales ... You're a foot too short!

Ames: What?

Ivan: You're a foot too short.

Ames: You mean at this weight I ought to be a foot taller.

Ivan: Definitely.

Ames: Well then I ought to lose weight.

Ivan: You ought to, but you won't.

Ames: Why not?

Ivan: I know your type. You overeat and won't take exercise.

Ames: But I would ...

Ivan: I don't know what to do with you – if I give you a diet, you won't stick to it.

interesting task you had to do this year?

- What was the most successful area in the past year?
- How do you feel you handled the reorganization in retrospect?
- What areas of your work would you say require more attention?
- What extra help do you need to improve those areas?
- What do you think you need to learn now to develop the job further?
- How have you found dealings with Accounts and Marketing have worked out?
- What have been the most difficult problems that you have faced?
- Where do you see your future in the company?
- How do you see this job developing?
- What would you say are the priorities for the next twelve months?

By using the open-ended questioning technique, you should get your subordinate to discuss the key areas of his job and how he has performed against the agreed standards. Where answers are vague or standards have not been met or have been vastly exceeded, you should react to these answers with a view to gaining further information, facts and views on why.

123

Ames: I'll try.

Ivan: If I give you exercises, you won't do them.

Ames: I'll do jogging.

Ivan: If I give you pills, you won't take them.

Ames: I would! I would! I promise you I would take pills.

Ivan: And I'm telling you you wouldn't.

Ames: ... Wouldn't I?

Ivan: You wouldn't.

Ames: Isn't there anything we can do?

Ivan: No, nothing. It's hopeless ... You'd best have your coronary now, while I'm here to deal with it. Well come on, come on, we haven't got all day.

Once again, the similarities between the doctor and the manager are demonstrated. The doctor should only discuss those things which can be remedied or improved. It is no good discussing an employee's personality defects (as you see them) with him. You discuss results and performance. 'You don't

Interpret performance

Ask yourself the following questions if:

a: performance is well in excess of standards –

  i: were the standards too low?

  ii: is he just a fantastic manager?

  iii: how are you going to develop him?

  iv: what extra training would he need for development?

  v: was performance high due to unforecasted market changes, i.e., luck running in your direction?

b: performance was well below standards –

i: were the standards too high?

ii: was he impeded from achieving the standards in the job and if so by whom?
1. you
2. another department
3. market forces outside his control

iii: was he below par in doing the job?

iv: if so, what are you going to do about it?

v: what training and guidance may be needed to improve his performance?

Before discussing your views on his performance with the employee, it is vital to have thought through the answers to the questions above. Before making your comments, it is a good idea to summarize what he has said so far. This gives a common launching pad for your views and also gives the subordinate the opportunity to correct any mistaken impressions you may have gained.

... and as for that supervisor, he gets right up my nostril ...!

have an aptitude for detail' is no more a management appraisal without facts and discussion of those facts than 'You are too short' is a medical opinion. When a doctor discusses a weight problem it is, or should be, as a problem, not as a criticism. Work difficulties can be diagnosed just as conscientiously as illnesses; and the response is more likely to be a good one if the tone of the exchange is helpful. Remember, when you are finding fault, to acknowledge successes as well. A doctor who says, 'I'm pleased with your weight loss, and I can see you are trying, but

Discuss performance, not personalities.

125

Concluding on a positive note

At the end of the interview you should summarize the main points made, reinforce the praise for work well done, go over the points for improvement and help to be given, then end the interview on a positive note of encouragement. The person should leave the interview with a clear mental picture of the situation. He should also be told what will happen to any interview notes and how many points arising will be followed up.

By handling the interview in this way, both you and the interviewee will achieve a satisfactory and positive dialogue with a thorough review of the year and clear action points for the future.

let's see if we can manage a little more,' will make more progress than one who simply says, 'You're too fat.' And never formulate your opinion, diagnosis or conclusion *before* you have both the necessary information and have given the employee an opportunity to explain points which may be relevant.

Alan's last appraisal interview was with William the Silent. As he tells Dr Evans, William was a nice enough person who listened, had done his homework but had one terrible fault. By the time of that interview Alan was pretty fed up with the whole company ...

William: Right, well, I'll arrange for you to go on that course then. And you want a spell away from line management some time ...
Ames: Soon.
William: Yes, right, jolly good, OK. Well, very pleased you can ... speak out like this, jolly healthy.
Ames: Are you satisfied with me?
William: ... Sorry?

That's all we can expect from you, I suppose ... OK, on your bike now ...

End the interview on a positive note.

Ames: Are you satisfied with *me*?

William: Oh yes. Yes, yes, yes. Er … Well, there is one … small thing …

Ames: What?

William: Well … the letter you wrote to the *Gazette*.

Ames: What was wrong with it?

William: Oh, it was just, well, it was, you know, well, a bit critical of our industry.

Ames: So you don't think firms like ours have a pollution problem?

William: Oh yes, oh yes. But don't you think 'capitalist rip-off' was a bit … strong?

Ames: It's true, isn't it?

William: Well, yes, yes, yes. It's a point of view, certainly.

Ames: *My* point of view.

William: Yes, exactly … but … if you'd written it from your home address rather than on company paper … ?

Ames: It's only coming from a named company that gives it any authority. Don't you think it's time this country woke up to the environmental facts of life?

William: Yes … Oh yes.

Ames: Unless the people who know have the guts to speak out, things will get worse and worse. Won't they?

William: Er, yes. Right.

Ames: Well there you are. We've agreed on something.

William: … Yes. I, er, I think I ought just to make a teeny mention of it in the report. Just, you know …

Ames: No.

William: Just a note? … Just a small … I know the Chairman felt …

Ames: Look, who's interviewing me – the Chairman or you?

William: I am. And I do feel that …

Ames: Fine. So long as I can write again to the *Gazette* saying you've officially

Discuss the employee's future

Asking the person to discuss his plans for the future and where he sees himself is a different exercise from your forecasting or giving a copper-bottomed guarantee of the individual's prospects and future. The latter may be beyond your control or it may be dangerous to commit yourself to making suggestions too far in advance. The person's performance and aptitude may change with time. What you should be doing is linking his views into your training and development plans without making hard and fast promises. Also, the individual's assessment of his potential and progression may be very different from yours. However, these assessments will help you to see which way his mind is working. If you see possibilities in his views, particularly if they involve a change in career, you should take notes for the future and give guidance and advice.

Agree a plan of action

An action plan should be based on the following:

1 How to use the person's strengths in the future.
2 How to achieve any improvements required.
3 How the person sees his development.

Agreeing an action plan is vital if the interview is not to end on a negative or inconclusive note.

You should be agreeing, at this stage of the interview, action for reversing a poor situation, even if the details have to be worked out at a later meeting. Your role at the appraisal is not just to discuss the past but also to show a way ahead and how you are going to support your subordinate to regain the required standard.

Likewise, with the person who is doing well, you need to be discussing with him ways of stretching and loading him over the next twelve months, otherwise he will be bored.

It is worth remembering that the person under review probably shines in certain parts of the work and needs some polishing in others. Most

censured me for telling the truth.

William: ... Well I suppose we could sort of unofficially record it ... gentleman's agreement ...

Ames: All right. So long as nothing goes in the report.

William: No ... right.

Dr Evans understands just what type of manager William was – a 'ducker' who wouldn't face up to anything. And he knows what kind of a doctor William would be ...

Ames: What do you mean, overweight?

William: ... Well, nothing, nothing.

Ames: Good. Now shut up.

William: Yes, but ... well, let me put it this way, your blood pressure is a bit high.

Ames: So?

William: Well ... I mean it's ... to be blunt ... it's phenomenally high.

Ames: I *like* it phenomenally high!

No good doctor shirks his responsibilities; nor does a good manager. They check case histories, collect information, make a diagnosis, discuss it as appropriate – and finally they agree a plan of action. Ethelred could have *no* plan of action through lack of forethought; Ivan would give a hectoring and irrelevant lecture on restructuring his employee's personality; and William would avoid action through weakness and a desire to avoid any possibility of unpleasantness. Where faults exist, recognize them, bring them out into the open and give yourself every chance to agree a plausible plan for improvement with your employee. Make it a *plausible* plan. Remember that you are looking for improvements which you may get, not sainthood which you won't. Tell an overweight businessman to jog for ten minutes a day and he'll probably do it. Tell him to run five miles and he'll stay in bed. Always follow up the agreed plan at regular intervals – don't leave it for next year's annual appraisal interview. And make a report immediately following the interview – then you'll have it properly recorded when next year comes round, and something to consult *through the year* as you check on the progress of the various items you have agreed.

people are not all good or all bad.

When discussing action plans, it is useful to get the person to volunteer what he thinks he needs to do and then get joint agreement on these points. In this way these plans will be more realistic and likely to be carried out, as the person is committed.

Record of the interview

So how do you fill in the appraisal form? During the interview you probably jotted down some notes. After the interview you should get down to completing the form immediately.

The best type of form is really a blank sheet of paper – which allows you scope to fill in relevant details. A person's performance can't be graded or marked with ticks or crosses in boxes – descriptions are required. A blank sheet of paper gives you this opportunity. This 'blank' will probably be used by Personnel and have certain organization data on it.

You will probably find it easier to complete the review under some headings, i.e. the key areas of the job, and comment on how these have been performed against the standards required. In the same way, you may like to use headings for any short-term priority tasks that you are reviewing.

An overall summary of performance is vital for inclusion on the form plus details of action plans, by when and how these should be implemented. You should sign this document and date it.

The exercise is then complete. Or is it? You really need a copy of the form so that you can monitor action plans and fulfil your part in helping the person with his development or his improvement plans. This is a vital part of making an appraisal an active and on-going exercise – rather than a once-per-year cut-and-dried interview with no follow-through. Appraisal is not a closed book. It should be the opening of new chapters.

Golden rules

Appraisal should be a dialogue.

Do your homework before the interview.

Create an informal atmosphere which assists in promoting discussion.

An employee expects, and should be given, the opportunity to discuss his work.

Discuss performance, not personalities.

Only discuss those things which can be remedied or improved.

Never reach a conclusion before giving the interviewee the chance to react.

Conclude on a positive note.

8 I'd like a word with you – the discipline interview

According to the *Oxford English Dictionary* discipline means, among other things, 'correction; chastisement; punishment … the mortification of the flesh by penance'. Possibly when you are in a bad mood this definition has a certain appeal. But for managers it is the other definitions from the dictionary which are more relevant:

1 Instructions imparted to disciples or scholars; teaching; learning; education; schooling.
2 Instruction having for its aim to form the pupil to proper conduct and action.

You can think of discipline in businesses as a combination of two things, one static and one dynamic. Static discipline is about having a clear and fair framework within which everyone can work: clear and fair rules on smoking, safety, timekeeping, and so on – and agreed standards of work for employees. Dynamic discipline is about ensuring that the rules and standards are kept and, if they are not, taking action to close the gap between required performance and actual performance.

Gaps like this can open up for a number of reasons: because the rules are so outdated that no one bothers with them; or because the rules and standards were never communicated to an employee – so ignorance is innocence, even if it is not bliss; or because someone chooses to flout the prescribed framework.

In the first instance the remedy is for management to take urgent action to revise and update its procedures and regulations; in the second, to look hard at its internal communications. But in the last case it is down to you, the individual's boss, to sort out the situation. So before you know what's happened, you find yourself conducting a discipline interview, whether you meant to or not, and whether or not you call it by that name.

It is usually one of three things that sparks off a discipline interview:

1 For some managers the need becomes obvious as a result of a logical analysis of someone's behaviour or performance against the accepted standards of his job.
2 For other managers it may be a simple relay action – your boss bawls you out for a mess-up on a particular project, so you decide to pass on his words, suitably amplified, to the individual who messed it up.

You pass on the boss's words, suitably amplified, to the individual who messed it up.

3 The third reason is that something snaps inside you, and you realize that you can't stomach Harry's abusiveness or Joan's lateness any longer, and that they are not responding to your 'hey, watch your language' or 'see you on time tomorrow' remarks.

If you are the type of person who falls into the first category, you can congratulate yourself. You have a greater chance of getting the interview off on the right foot. If you have found yourself in the second or third categories, beware! Remember the adage about fools rushing in. Your temper and instant response to a situation will probably cause trouble. Temper breeds aggression in others – therefore a satisfactory conversation is unlikely. Also, if you instantly leap into an interview you will be breaking the first cardinal rule of interviewing: be prepared.

If you are in a temper you are quite likely to forego the refinements of privacy and bawl the person out in front of others. However wrong the person is, all you are doing is making a martyr out of him and a fool of yourself in front of the rest of the staff. So before you say that pregnant phrase, 'I'd like a word with you,' what should you do?

First and foremost, remember that future performance is your real concern, so keep the bulk of the interview pointing forward and avoid excessive argument and recrimination about the past.

Next, think of yourself as trying to repair a gap, the gap between someone's required performance and his actual performance. There are three stages to a discipline interview:

1 Establishing the gap.
2 Exploring the reasons for the gap.
3 Eliminating the gap.

Let's take establishing the gap first. That's the part that defeats our old friend Ethelred the Unready. Ethelred's boss has a complaint …

Ramsay: I've been looking at the time sheets for the service engineers. The call rates are slipping – the lazy bastards. Especially Jeffries.
Ethelred: Right. I'll read him the riot act straight away.

George Jeffries is summoned to the Presence:

Ethelred: George, come in and sit down.

Establish the gap

Part of this exercise needs to take place before you decide to have your heart-to-heart with the person.
You need to:

a: check the facts on his performance
b: check the facts on your requirements.

Both steps are vital.
To check the facts on his performance you must find out all the details of the problem. You may need to refer to all or some of the following:

1 His personal files (particularly if you are a new boss in the section).

2 His clock cards, flexible-time records, the signing-in book and time sheets.
3 The customer complaints file.
4 His unfinished work.
5 The reject file/book.
6 His sickness and absence record.
7 Your colleagues who come into contact with him.
8 His work sheets.
9 His record cards.
10 His work files.
11 His correspondence.
12 The Personnel Department, for any additional information and background on the individual.
13 His job description.
14 His budgets – and the monthly management accounts.

To check the facts on your requirements you must:

1 Read the company rules covering the situation.
2 Re-read the job description – but this time in conjunction with the agreed standards of performance for each task.
3 Remind yourself when you last stated your operational requirements to your staff, and check if the person concerned was present.
4 Check the performance records of the others who work with him, to make sure that he is significantly below the average.
5 Look at the financial plans for the department.

Now then, let me tell you what this is about … as soon as I've found your time sheets. Susan must have filed them. Now … oh, we need your job cards, don't we … there we are. Now George, you're not really pulling your weight, are you? Look at the figures.

George: What's wrong with them?

Ethelred: These time sheets and job cards aren't filled out properly. They're very important, we can't schedule calls …

George: I didn't know they mattered.

Ethelred: Of course they matter. What do you think we have them for? Look at that one – it's got beer stains all over it. I mean, it's obviously concocted in a pub, isn't it?

George: Where do you want me to do them, in church? I didn't know you cared so much about the bloody forms. I thought it was better to get on with the job. But if you want me to fill in the forms, I'll fill in the forms! But you've never mentioned it before, have you?

Ethelred: Not as such, perhaps. But I should have thought it was obvious that we couldn't schedule …

George: Well it isn't. When old Harry was the supervisor, he didn't care about the forms.

Ethelred: Well I didn't know that, did I?

First point: in order to establish the gap between standards and performance you must check the facts on the standard for the job. Then you have another pitfall to avoid:

Ethelred: I'm sorry George, but your call rate's not up to standard.

George: What standard? How many more calls do the others make, then?

Ethelred: Well, I don't know the exact

figures. But look at this ... completely blank.

George: That was the afternoon you called us in for a meeting. Next?

Ethelred: How about that! One call in the whole day?

George: The job took all day, didn't it!

Ethelred: Look, the point is, I *know* your call rate's not good enough. I'm going to give you a warning.

George: And I'm going to talk to my shop steward.

Second point: as well as checking the facts on standards, you also have to check the facts on performance. Otherwise you can't establish that there's a gap between them. But suppose Ethelred had done his homework ...

Wow, a Royal Flush!

Ethelred: George, is there any reason that these time sheets and job cards are not filled in properly?

George: Better to do the job than waste the day filling in forms.

Have the facts available.

135

Ethelred: But we waste time if we can't
schedule the calls properly. And we
can't schedule if we don't know which
jobs have been done. We can't send the
bills either.

George: Old Harry never seemed
bothered about it.

Ethelred: That's one of the things we've
got to put right. From now on these
forms must be accurately completed.

George: I don't forget very often.

Ethelred: Well, actually you do. Less than
half of these are properly filled in.

George: None of the lads bother about
them.

Ethelred: That's partly true, but they're
all better than this. I've been through all
the time sheets and yours definitely
contain the least information.

George: I do the job all right though,
don't I?

Ethelred: You could be one of our best
engineers, but your call rate is a bit low.
Tell me, is there any reason why you
never call in after three o'clock for
unallocated calls?

George: My allocated calls take all day.

Ethelred: Always?

George: Nearly always.

Ethelred: Every housewife is nearly
always in whenever you call? You see, if
you don't do your full quota it puts
extra strain on everybody else. Do you
see what I mean? We'll say no more
about it, because you may have thought
I was happy with Harry's system. So
this is just an informal warning. But in
future these time sheets and job cards
must be completed accurately.
Otherwise I shall have to give you a
formal warning.

George: I'll talk to my shop steward.

Ethelred: That's fine. All these
procedures are agreed with the union.

But you just have to do this and there's nothing to worry about.

So that's it. He had the facts on the standards of the job. He had the facts on the actual performance. So it was possible to be very specific about the gap between the two.

Now let's look at another old friend, Ivan the Terrible. His weak point is exploring the reasons for the gap.

Ivan: Ah, there you are, Joan. Late again.
Joan: I'm sorry, but …
Ivan: Well sorry's no good, is it? This is the third time in two weeks. The company doesn't exist for your convenience, you know. Everyone else gets here on time. Look! All here, working away. Doing your work as well as theirs. It's not fair, is it?
Joan: No, but …
Ivan: No, it is not fair. What have you got to say for yourself?
Joan: Nothing.
Ivan: Nothing? Well, if you turn up late again you needn't bother to come back.

To start with, you should never reprimand people 'off the cuff'. The best approach is to fix a time to see the person concerned, saying you want to discuss his or her work, time-keeping or whatever, and ensure that the meeting is conducted in private. The discipline interview is not a spectator sport, and nosey-parkers won't help either of you to resolve the situation. Constant interruptions can give the person concerned the idea that you are not really bothered, and that in any case you are too busy to care.

Fixing a time means that your temper can cool, and you can prepare yourself before the interview. Don't put things off indefinitely, though; breaches of discipline should be

Explore the reasons

The only way to do this is to get the interviewee to talk the situation through. Not so easy? No, not always, but you will compound your difficulties if you don't use the interviewer's stock in trade – open-ended questions.

These are questions that begin with: what, when, where, how and who. For instance, 'What were your reasons for being late this morning?' or 'What's the trouble?'

A 'why' question is also open-ended. But if the temperature is a little hot, the 'why' question, which is inclined to make a person justify himself, may just blow the lid off the conversation.

You must listen to the answers given and find out the following:

1 Is the problem just a way of getting attention? i.e. the person has a grievance.
2 Is the problem caused by a personal difficulty? i.e. poor time-keeping because of a sick child, or marriage problems.
3 Is the problem due to the fact that the person needs more help and training to do the job?

4 Is it because the rules are hopelessly out of date and impossible to work within?

5 Is it a genuine discipline problem?

6 Is the cause a clash of personalities in the work group?

7 Is the problem because the company has not communicated its requirements properly, or is there a genuine lack of clarity about what is required?

discussed within twenty-four hours of the event.

Your initial approach is crucial. Apart from being clear about the facts, you must constantly remind yourself to stick to them. Stay calm and don't allow any prejudice or animosity to show. Because of his irritation with her, Ivan has almost sacked Joan, who has been a good worker for years. That's why it's so important to explore the reasons for the gap ... Why was Joan late? Can Ivan repair the damage:

Ivan: Now, Joan, perhaps I was a bit short

THE HARRY STROPWICK ROLLICKING

GET YOUR TICKETS HERE →

The discipline interview is not a spectator sport.

with you this morning. I didn't really give you a chance to speak, did I? Well now's your chance.

Joan: Well, you see, I ...

Ivan: I'm like that sometimes. I jump down people's throats. I don't mean to, but I do. I know I do. I bloody *terrify* some of them ... Well, come on Joan, get on with it!

Joan: What do you want me to say?

Ivan: Why are you behaving so irres-
ponsibly lately? Well not ... but why are
you letting us down? Behaving so badly.

The exploration must be a real one. That
means asking open questions, not loaded
ones. Open questions are the ones that invite
a full explanation, rather than a short, defen-
sive reply. They are particularly useful when
dealing with sullen, silent types. Just ask your
question and shut up. By the normal rules of
conversation, you will get an answer, even if
the answer does take some time to come out.

From your homework you will have the
facts of the case, but a discipline interview is
not just a one-sided conversation, a 'show
trial'. The person must be encouraged to
state his case and you must attempt to create
an atmosphere in which he will do this. Don't
jump to the conclusion that you are dealing
with a discipline problem in the first place.
Keep your mind open – then the questions
will be too. Let's look at Ivan approaching the
problem properly:

Ivan: Ah, Joan, there you are.
Joan: I'm sorry, but ... I can't cope ...
Ivan: Now what's the trouble?
Joan: I'll go and start work.
Ivan: No, I want to know why you're late.
Joan: I'm tired.
Ivan: Yes?
Joan: Well ... I live with my old Mum,
and I look after her without any help,
but the week before last she had a nasty
fall. She's eighty-one, you know, and
she can't be left alone. I don't want her
to go to a home so I arranged for a
home help to come every morning at
eight o'clock, but sometimes she's late
and I have to wait for her.
Ivan: Yes. Well, you sort things out at
home, and if you have to be late a few
mornings we'll manage for a bit.

By listening, Ivan has discovered that this *isn't really a discipline problem at all*. Which gives him the option of adjusting, for the time being, the standards he expects of Joan.

So when you're exploring the reasons for the gap, don't jump to conclusions. One, ask open questions. Two, listen patiently for the answers, and three, check that it really is a discipline problem. If you do make exceptions, *make sure you tell the others*.

Finally, *eliminate the gap*. That's William the Silent's big problem. He sees the situation as a struggle for dominance – and he's frightened he's going to lose. He has a problem with Jonathan ...

Jonathan: You wanted to see me?
William: Er ... yes. Well, how're things?
Jonathan: Fine, how's things with you?
William: Yes ... fine.
Jonathan: So we're both fine. Is there anything else? I'm fairly busy at the moment.
William: Well, just a couple of things that I ought to mention.
Jonathan: What?
William: I'm coming to them. Now in my position as Acting Head of Sales, I have to ... thank you for coming here ... especially as this is in the nature of a dis ... dis ...
Jonathan: Dis what?
William: ... Discipline interview. Well, not exactly discipline, but I mean ... er ... we're all grown men, but rules are rules.
Jonathan: Are you saying that I'm not doing my job properly?
William: Would you like a coffee?

William is blurring everything by turning it into a 'who's in charge?' struggle. He should focus on the facts. But that is not everything ...

Eliminate the gap

Assuming you are satisfied that the person's performance is below standard or he is breaking the rules, and a grievance or personal problem is not the cause, then you must agree on an improvement plan.

To do this you will have to remind him of what is expected, and why this standard or volume of work is important, or why the rules must be kept. Ask him what he is going to do about it. Then you must tell him how you will help him to achieve this work standard, or the required volume of work, by, for example:

more training (off the job)
more training (on the job)
more information

In all cases you must fix a review date and explain what the procedural consequences will be if there is no improvement by this date. You should also make it clear that you want him to succeed, and that you will be giving him as much help and encouragement as you possibly can during this review time.

Jonathan: You wanted to see me.
William: Yes. Just about a couple of
things.
Jonathan: I'm very busy at the moment.
William: You seem to be er ...
overspending your budget.
Jonathan: How do you mean?
William: Your budget is over the ... how
shall I put it? ... Spent. Over is what
your budget is spent. It's supposed to
be £100,000 per quarter. But last
quarter you spent over £120,000.
Jonathan: That's all right. My sales have
gone up 20 per cent.
William: I beg your pardon?
Jonathan: My budget was allocated as 25
per cent of the expected sales. My sales
have gone up 20 per cent.
William: But your budget is expressed as
a figure, not as a percentage of
sales.
Jonathan: It's all very well for you people
up here in your penthouse suites. You
just sit here shuffling papers around.
My salesmen are down there making
money for the company.
William: I do know a bit about it, you
know – I was in Sales for six years. And
now that I'm Acting Head of Sales, well
... I'm in charge. I'd like to make this
perfectly clear ...

William has focussed on the facts all right
but has not *stuck* to them. He has allowed
himself to be diverted from a perfectly
reasonable point and to become distracted by
what is essentially irrelevant. Let us look at
how he *should* have dealt with things:

William: Jonathan, the point is that you
spent £120,000, instead of £100,000.
Jonathan: Yes, but I think my budget
should be expressed in percentage
terms.

William: That's not the way this company works.

Jonathan: It's the way I work.

William: Are you saying that you can't work with this company.

Jonathan: No, I didn't mean that.

William: We work to agreed budgets. We have a set of agreed standards which you accepted when you joined us, didn't you? So either you or the standards have got to change.

Jonathan: Fine. We'll change the standards.

William: I can't change them. If you want to, you must go to the very top and convince them. Meantime, we have to work with the standards as they are. So I want you to work out a plan showing how you're going to make up the £20,000 in the next quarter.

Jonathan: I can't make up £20,000 in one quarter.

William: Can you do it in two?

Jonathan: I can try.

So that's another point. As soon as you've got the facts in focus, move on to the future. Agree a target for future performance, to put things right and make sure the follow-up is established:

William: So you can come back on Friday week?

Jonathan: What for?

William: To show me your plan for cutting £20,000 off the next two quarters' expenditure.

Jonathan: And if I can't?

William: Then it passes out of my hands. I'd have to speak to the Managing Director about it. I'm sorry, but those are the rules.

Jonathan: Friday week? I'll see what I can do.

William: Then we'll look at it again at the end of the month, just to make sure it's working properly.

William the Resolute has remembered to fix a date for reviewing the situation, and you, like him, should explain what the procedural consequences will be if there is no improvement by this date. You should also make it clear that you want him to succeed, and that you will be giving him as much help and encouragement as you possibly can during this review time.

So that's it:

1 Establish the gap. Check the facts on standards, check the facts on performance and agree the area of the gap.
2 Explore the gap. Ask open questions, listen for the answers and check that it really is a discipline problem and not a grievance or hardship case in disguise.
3 Eliminate the gap. Focus on the facts, look to the future and agree a target, and then fix a review date.

Golden rules

Be prepared.

Future performance is your first concern.

Never reprimand 'off the cuff'.

A discipline interview is not a spectator sport.

Ask your question and shut up.

Don't prejudge the case – you may discover you are not dealing with a discipline problem at all.

When you make exceptions in individual cases, tell the others.

Know and explain procedural aspects and consequences.

Focus on facts; stick to facts.

Agree targets for future performance.